Training of defensive and semi-offensive cooperative defense strategies for handball teams
60 exercises – From 1-on-1 to small group and team defense

Introduction

A good defense is a prerequisite for modern team handball. The intention is not only to prevent goals but also to actively win the ball and subsequently initiate a fast attack. The offense should permanently be put under pressure and forced to make mistakes.

The exercises in this collection initially deal with the individual basics of defense play. Individual and position-specific training marks the starting point for subsequent cooperative defense play and allows for choosing the appropriate defense system. The basics both include exercises on legwork, 1-on-1 defense and covering the pivot in combination with fast adjustment to subsequent actions as well as blocking and anticipating on the wing positions of a proactive defense system.

The second part of the collection deals with cooperative small group defense play and focuses on handing over/taking over attacking players along the defense line (width of defense) and on making agreements when defending against the pivot.

The third chapter introduces cooperative team defense in 6-0, 5-1, 3-2-1, and 4-2 defense systems along with possible variants.

Get inspired by the exercises, develop your own defense concepts, and make use of the individual strengths of your defense players for optimal cooperation.

Publishing information
1st English edition released on 15 Aug 2018
German original edition released on 09 Mai 2018

Published by DV Concept
Editors, design, and layout: Jörg Madinger, Elke Lackner
Proofreading and English translation: Nina-Maria Nahlenz

ISBN: 978-3-95641-214-1

This publication is listed in the catalogue of the **German National Library**. Please refer to http://dnb.de for bibliographic data.

The work and its components are protected by copyright. No reprinting, photomechanical reproduction, storing or processing in electronic systems without the publisher's written permission.

Contents:

No.	Name	Players	Difficulty level	Page
Category: Individual basics				
1. General exercises on legwork and basic defense movements				
1	Basic defense training with ropes	4	★	6
2	Goalkeeper warm-up shooting with defense legwork	8	★	7
3	Actively stepping forward towards the ball holder 3-on-4	2	★★	9
4	Reaction training with actively stepping forward towards the ball holder	8	★★	10
5	Stepping forward and moving backward during the goalkeeper warm-up shooting	8	★★★	12
6	Stepping forward and moving backward on the left/right back positions	8	★★★	13
2. Exercises on physical contact				
7	Pushing attacking players out of the 6-meter zone/Preventing a breakthrough	8	★★	14
8	Preventing an attacking player from breaking through 2-on-1	8	★★	16
9	Preventing an attacking player from breaking through 3-on1 or 2-on-1	8	★★	17
3. 1-on-1 defense play				
10	Ball familiarization 1-on-1	3	★★	19
11	Basic movements and 1-on-1	3	★★	20
12	1-on-1 exercise with fast adjustment and without a ball	9	★★	21
13	1-on-1 exercise with fast adjustment and without a ball 2	9	★★	22
14	4 times 1-on-1	8	★★	23
15	1-on-1 with a preparatory exercise	8	★★	24
16	Several 1-on-1 actions in a row	8	★★	25
17	Continuous 1-on-1 exercise with fast adjustment	10	★★	27
18	1-on-1 following a preparatory athletics exercise	10	★★★★	28
4. Covering the pivot				
19	Covering the pivot	6	★	30
20	Playing outside and inside a circle and covering the pivot	9	★★	31
21	Shielding off the pivot	8	★★	32
22	1-on-1 and shielding off the pivot	12	★★★	33
23	Basic movements, 1-on-1, and covering the pivot on the left and right back positions	8	★★★	34

Training of defensive and semi-offensive cooperative defense strategies for handball teams
60 exercises – From 1-on-1 to small group and team defense

No.	Name	Players	Difficulty level	Page
5. Blocking in agreement with the goalkeeper				
24a	Blocking the throwing hand goal corner while moving	10	★★★	36
24b	Blocking the short goal corner while moving	10	★★★	37
25	Blocking following a 1-on-1 action	10	★★★	38
26	Blocking after a 1-on-1 action with the attacking players crossing	10	★★★	39
27a	Blocking in agreement with the goalkeeper	10	★★★★	40
27b	Blocking in agreement with the goalkeeper	10	★★★★	41
6. Active wing position defense				
28	Pressing on the wing positions	8	★★	43
29	Active wing player on the opposite side	8	★★	44
30	Pressing on the wing positions and active wing player on the opposite side	8	★★	45
31	1-on-1 pressing on the wing positions	9	★★	46
32	Defending 1-on-2 on the wing positions	8	★★★	47
Category: Small group work				
1. Cooperation across the width of defense				
33	2-on-2 with quick switching	6	★★	48
34	3-on-3	10	★★	50
35	3-on-3 switch game	9	★★	52
36	1-on-1 and 2-on-2 combination	7	★★	53
37	2-on-2 with fast adjustment	7	★★	55
2. Cooperation throughout the depth of defense				
38	2-on-2 – Defense against back position player and pivot	8	★★	56
39	2-on-2 defense against the Russian screen in two variants	9	★★	57
40	1-on-1 and 2-on-2 throughout the depth of defense	10	★★	58
41	Defending against the wing position and back position players, and the pivot 3-on-3	10	★★	60
Category: Team cooperation				
1. 6-0 defense				
42	5-on-5 – Defending and supporting 1-on-1	11	★★★	61
43	Defending against the pivot in the center block (outnumbered defense)	9	★★★	62
44	Defending in the center block of a defensively acting 6-0 defense system	13	★★★	64

No.	Name	Players	Difficulty level	Page
45	Defending in the center block of an offensively acting 6-0 defense system	11	★★★	65
46a	Defending on the wing positions of an offensively acting 6-0 defense system – preparatory exercise	10	★★★	67
46b	Defending on the wing positions of an offensively acting 6-0 defense system – main exercise	10	★★★	70
47	Defending in an offensively acting 6-0 defense system – Combination of exercises 45, 46a, and 46b	11	★★★	72
2. 5-1 defense				
48	Defending on the center front position of a 5-1 defense system	8	★★	73
49	Defending in the center block of a 5-1 defense system	11	★★★	74
50	5-1 defense system with offensively acting wing player on the opposite side in a 5-on-5 game	11	★★★	76
51	5-1 defense with offensively acting wing player on the opposite side in a 6-on-6 game	13	★★★	78
3. 3-2-1 defense				
52	Preparatory exercise for the 3-2-1 defense system in a 3-on-3 game	10	★★	79
53	Preparatory exercise for the 3-2-1 defense system in a 4-on-4 game	8	★★	80
54	Preparatory exercise – Switching to a 4-2 defense system	12	★★★	81
55	3-2-1 defense with switching to a 4-2 system due to a second pivot	13	★★★	82
56	3-2-1 defense without switching to a 4-2 system despite a second pivot – preparatory 3-on-3 exercise	11	★★★	84
57	3-2-1 defense without switching to a 4-2 system despite a second pivot – 4-on-4	9	★★★	85
4. 4-2 defense				
58	Movement paths of the defense front row	10	★★★	87
59	Movement paths of the defense front row and the offensively acting wing player on the opposite side	10	★★★	88
60	4-2 team defense	13	★★★	89

Editor's note

Further reference books published by DV Concept

Training of defensive and semi-offensive cooperative defense strategies for handball teams
60 exercises – From 1-on-1 to small group and team defense

Key:

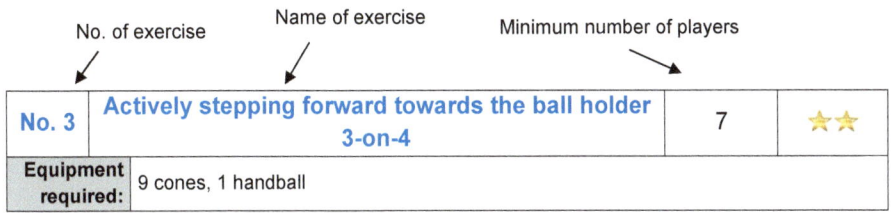

| No. of exercise | Name of exercise | Minimum number of players |

No. 3	**Actively stepping forward towards the ball holder 3-on-4**	7	★★
Equipment required:	9 cones, 1 handball		

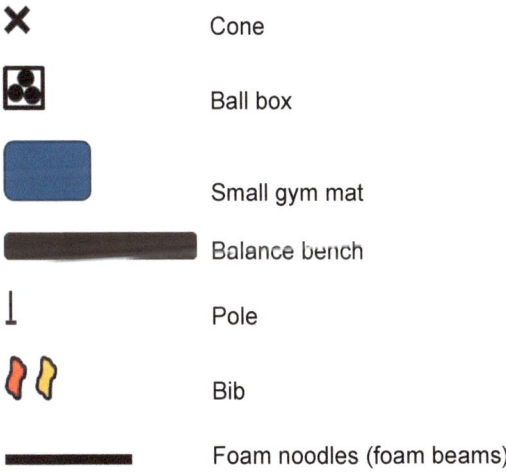

✗	Cone
⬛	Ball box
▬	Small gym mat
▬▬	Balance bench
⊥	Pole
🦵🦵	Bib
▬▬▬	Foam noodles (foam beams)

The exercises are divided into the following difficulty levels:

★: This exercise can be done both by beginners and well-advanced players and is intended to develop basic defense skills.

★★: This exercise requires some experience but may be done by players of all age groups with appropriate adaptation.

★★★: This exercise is more complex and requires proficiency in the basic skills.

★★★★: This exercise is very complex and should be done by well-trained players in the competitive areas only who fulfill the athletic requirements. Four stars are awarded to exercises also when a specific defense system is required that should be practiced by older age groups only.

Training of defensive and semi-offensive cooperative defense strategies for handball teams
60 exercises – From 1-on-1 to small group and team defense

Category: Individual basics

1. General exercises on legwork and basic defense movements

No. 1	Basic defense training with ropes	4	★
Equipment required: 4 cones and 2 ropes (without handles) per team of 2			

Setting:
- The players make groups of 2.
- Define one playing field per group with cones or use existing field markings on the floor.

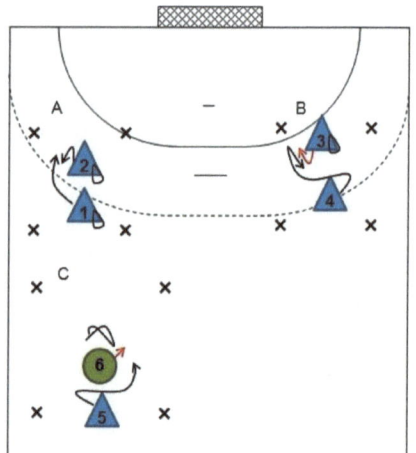

Course 1 (A):
- Each player has a rope folded once or twice and put it into the waistband of his pants on the backside.
- Upon the coach's whistle, the pairs start simultaneously, and each player tries to pull out the rope of his opponent's pants.
- If a player succeeds before the coach whistles again (after 20 seconds), he gets a point. The other player must do 10 jumping jacks.
- After the first round, one player of each team changes to the next field clockwise and the course starts over with new pairs.
- Who has scored highest in the end?

Course 2 (B):
- Only one player per team has a rope folded twice and put it into the waistband of his pants on the backside.
- Upon the coach's whistle, all the players without a rope start simultaneously and try to steal their teammate's rope as fast as possible.
- If a player succeeds, he calls out "STOP".
- The player who first calls out "STOP" gets a point.
- The players without a rope change to the next field clockwise and the course starts over.
- As soon as all the players without a rope have played one time against each player with a rope, the player who has scored highest wins the game.
- Now switch the tasks, i.e. the players without a rope in the first round now take the ropes; the other players try to be the first stealing the rope in each field.

Course 3: (C):
- Put a folded rope on the floor in the center of each field.
- One player per field starts as the defending player, one as the attacking player.
- Upon the coach's whistle, the attacking players try to pick up the rope as fast as possible.
- The defending players try to prevent this for as long as possible.
- After 20 seconds, the coach whistles again. All attacking players who managed to pick up the rope and all defending players who successfully defended the rope (rope is still on the floor) get a point.
- Now switch the tasks (attacking/defending player) in each field.
- After the second round, one player per field moves to the next field clockwise and the course starts over with new pairs.
- Who has scored highest in the end?

No. 2	Goalkeeper warm-up shooting with defense legwork	8	★
Equipment required: Sufficient number of handballs			

Setting:
- Two players start as the defending players, the other players stand at the 9-meter line, each holding a handball.

Course:
- ① starts on the left wing position, makes a step forward and touches the ball held by ▲1, quickly moves back to the 6-meter line, makes a step forward again and touches the ball held by ▲3, etc. (A).
- ② starts the course a bit delayed on the right side (B).
- A soon as ▲1 has touched the ball, ▲1 approaches the goal and shoots at the left side of the goal (C).

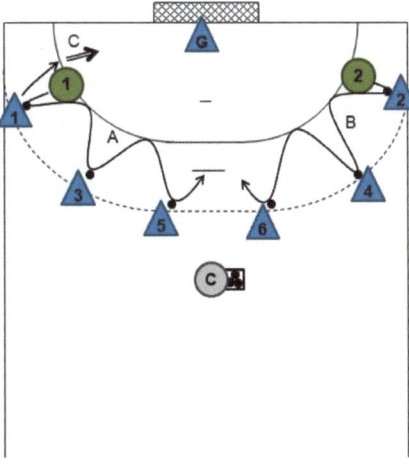

(Figure 1)

- Afterwards, 2 shoots at the right side of the goal (D), once 2 has touched the ball.
- The other players subsequently shoot at the left and right side of the goal alternately (E) and as instructed (top, bottom, middle).
- As soon as 1 has touched each handball, he receives a pass from the coach (F) and also shoots at the left side of the goal (H); 2 receives another pass from the coach (G) and shoots at the right side of the goal and as instructed (J).

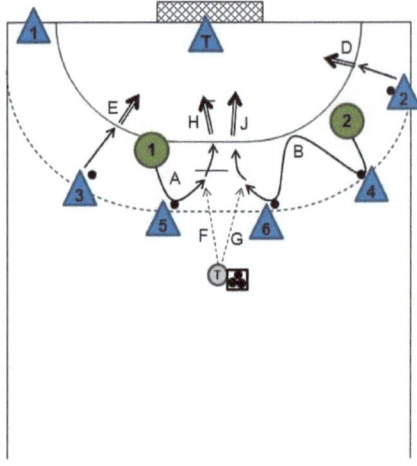

(Figure 2)

⚠ Change the defending players for the next shooting round.

⚠ Make sure that the defending players move back to the 6-meter line after they touched the ball and before they start running towards the next ball.

⚠ The shooting players should try to create a rhythm for the goalkeeper and make sure that he is able to reach and save the shots. They probably must delay their action a bit after the defending player has touched the respective handball.

(Figure 3)

(Figure 4)

No. 3	Actively stepping forward towards the ball holder 3-on-4	2	★★
Equipment required: 9 cones, 1 handball			

Setting:
- Put four cone goals diagonally in the corners and one cone into the center of a suitable playing field (see figure).

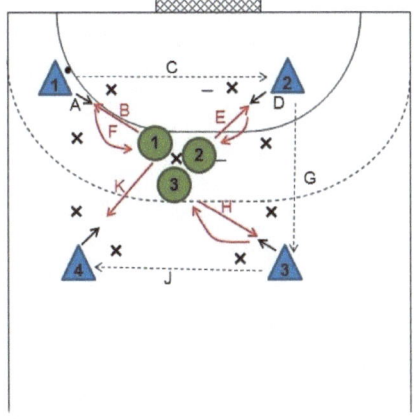

(Figure 1)

Course:
- ① makes a piston movement towards the gap between the two cones (A). ① steps forward actively into his movement path (B) and slightly pushes him back.
- ① passes to ② (C) who makes a piston movement towards the gap between the cones (D) and feints a stem shot. ② steps forward into the movement path of ② (E) and slightly pushes him back.
- ② passes to ③ (G), who makes a piston movement towards the gap between the cones. ③ steps forward into the movement path of ③ (H) and slightly pushes him back.

(Figure 2)

- In the meantime, ① has moved back and touched the cone in the center (F).
- ③ passes to ④ who starts the piston movement (J) and ① steps forward into the movement path of ④ (K), etc.

Variant:
- Allow return passes. The three defending players must clearly agree upon who is in charge of the respective attacking payer.

⚠ The players who do the piston movement must give the defending players sufficient time to get into physical contact and then play a quick pass into the running path of the next teammate.

⚠ The defending players should step forward quickly and then move back towards the cone in the center immediately.

⚠ Switch the defending players at regular intervals.

No. 4	Reaction training with actively stepping forward towards the ball holder	8	★★

Equipment required: One cone and one handball per team of 4

Setting:
- The players make teams of 4.
- Put one cone per team on the floor.

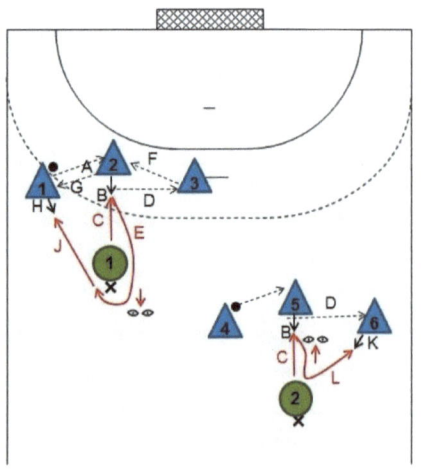

Course 1:
- ①, ②, and ③ stand next to each other while keeping a distance to the cone (② might stand a bit further in the back); ① stands next to the cone (see figure)

  ① plays the initial pass to ② (A), who makes a slight piston movement (B) and feints a stem shot.

- ① steps forward into the movement path of ② (C) and gets into physical contact while maintaining a defending body posture (one hand towards the opponent's throwing hand, the other hand towards his hip) and slightly pushes ② back.

- ② passes to ③ (D). The three attacking players keep playing quick passes (F and G) while ① runs around the cone (E), with passes from ① to ③ and vice versa being allowed. ① runs forward, his view is not in direction of the attacking players.

- As soon as ① turns around at the cone, the player who is about to receive the ball next, makes a slight piston movement and feints a stem shot (H). ① steps forward towards his movement path (J) and slightly pushes him back.
- Afterwards, ① runs around the cone again and the players repeat the course several times.
- After eight actions, the players switch positions.
- The other teams of 4 do the drill in parallel.

⚠ ① must check who has the ball once he has arrived at the cone in order to step forward towards the respective player.

Course 2:
- The basic course remains the same.
- After the initial pass, ▲5 makes a slight piston movement (R), ② steps forward into his movement path (C) and pushes him back.
- ▲5 passes to ▲6 (D), and the attacking players may keep passing freely.
- ② now moves backward to the cone while observing the attacking players.
- As soon as one of the attacking players bounces the ball once, makes a piston movement, and feints a shot (K), ② immediately changes his running direction, runs forward (L) – even if he had not arrived at the cone yet –, steps forward towards the attacking player's movement path and pushes him back.
- After eight actions, the players switch positions again.

| No. 5 | Stepping forward and moving backward during the goalkeeper warm-up shooting | 8 | ★★★ |

Equipment required: 3 cones, 2 ball boxes with sufficient number of handballs

Setting:
- Position three cones as shown in the figure.

Course:
- ① starts to dribble and feints a stem shot (A).
- ① steps forward into the movement path of ① and slightly pushes him back (B).
- Afterwards, ① runs around the left cone (C), receives a pass from ① into his running path (D), and eventually shots at the left side of the goal as instructed (hands, top, bottom) (E).

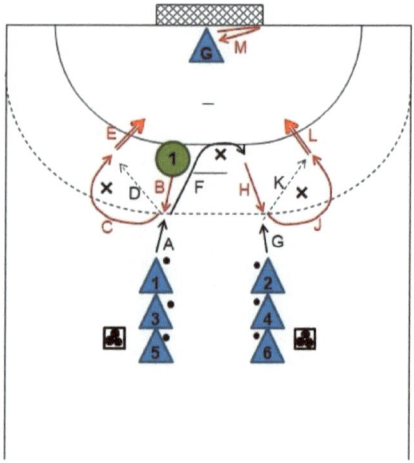

- ① becomes the next defending player, runs around the cone at the 6-meter line (F), and steps forward towards the movement of ② (H), who has started a piston movement on the right side (G).
- As soon as ① has pushed ② back slightly, ① runs around the cone on the right (J), receives a pass from ② into his running path (K), and shoots at the right side of the goal as instructed (L).
- And so on.

⚠ The players should perform a clear-cut defense action before they quickly adjust and start the shooting action.

| No. 6 | **Stepping forward and moving backward on the left/right back positions** | 8 | ★★★ |

Equipment required: 6 cones, 2 handballs

Setting:
- Define the running path with six cones as shown in the figure.

Course:

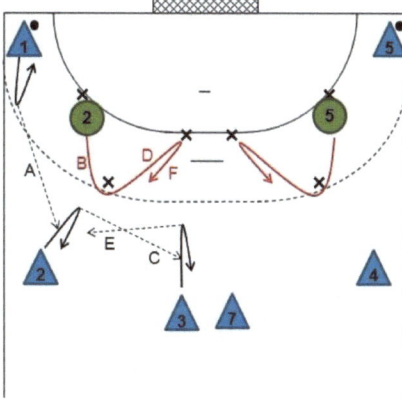

- 1 starts the piston movement on the wing position and passes into the running path of 2 (A).
- 2 does the same running movement in parallel towards the cone (B).
- 2 makes a piston movement in direction of the cone and passes the ball to 3 into his running path (C).
- 2 runs around the foremost cone and then back to the backmost cone (D).
- 3 makes a piston movement in direction of the goal and passes the ball back to 2 (E).
- 2 runs back again and around the foremost cone (F).
- 2 passes the ball back to the wing player and the course starts over.
- 7, 4, 5, and 5 do the same course in parallel on the other side.

⚠ 2 must coordinate his running movement in such a way that he is stepping forward as soon as 2 receives the pass and moves backward immediately after he passed the ball.

⚠ 1, 2, and 3 must move back again immediately after they played the pass so that they are ready to start the piston movement for the next action.

2. Exercises on physical contact

No. 7	Pushing attacking players out of the 6-meter zone/Preventing a breakthrough	8	★★
Equipment required: In course 2: 1 cone and 2-3 handballs			

Course 1 (figure 1):
- Make two teams.
- Both teams start at the 6-meter zone; one team defending, the other team attacking.
- Upon the coach's command, the defending players try to push the attacking players out of the 6-meter zone as fast as possible by getting into physical contact (A) and controlled pushing movements (C).
  The other players try to stay in the 6-meter zone for as long as possible (B). They must not enter the 6-meter zone once they have been pushed out, however.
- Stop the time as soon as all players have been pushed out of the 6-meter zone.
- Switch tasks afterwards. Which team has pushed their opponents out of the 6-meter zone fastest?

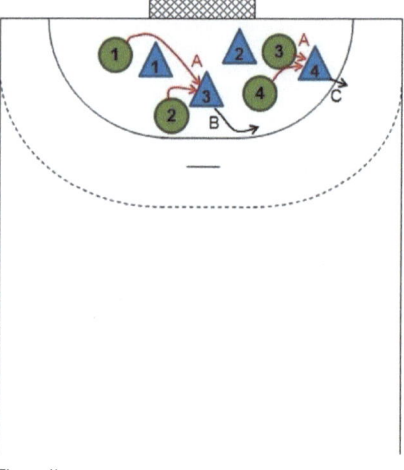
(Figure 1)

The defending players may collaborate and develop strategies on their own.

⚠ The defending players should not push but rather force their opponents to move (get into physical contact and move their opponent away by using bent arms and doing quick steps).

Course 2 (figure 2):

- Make two teams.
- The attacking players have two handballs and start in the goal. The defending players start in the 6-meter zone.
- Make the field smaller with a cone, so that not the entire 6-meter zone is available for playing (see figure).
  Upon the coach's starting signal, the two attacking players with the ball try to cross the 6-meter zone as fast as possible (A) and to leave it (C) (while holding the ball in their hands).
- The defending players try to stop the attacking players from breaking through and out of the 6-meter zone by collaborating and by getting into physical contact (B).
- If an attacking player manages to break through (C), he passes the ball to a teammate in the goal (D) who then also tries to break through.
- As soon as all players except the last one have left the 6-meter zone, stop the time and switch tasks.
- Which defense team manages to prevent the attacking players from breaking through for the longest time?

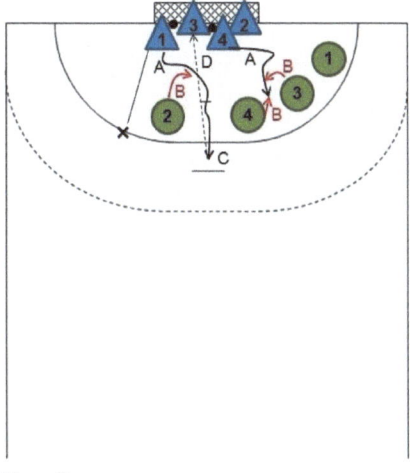
(Figure 2)

⚠ Define the playing field with a cone and according to the players' level of performance.

⚠ The attacking players may play a return pass to the next player in the goal anytime if they don't manage to leave the 6-meter zone. If this is the case, they must go back into the goal, however.

⚠ The defending players must maintain a one meter's distance to the goal and must not interrupt return passes nor the attacking players from starting their action.

| No. 8 | Preventing an attacking player from breaking through 2-on-1 | 8 | ★★ |

Equipment required: Two cones and one handball per team of 4

Setting:
- Define the finish lines with cones (see figure).

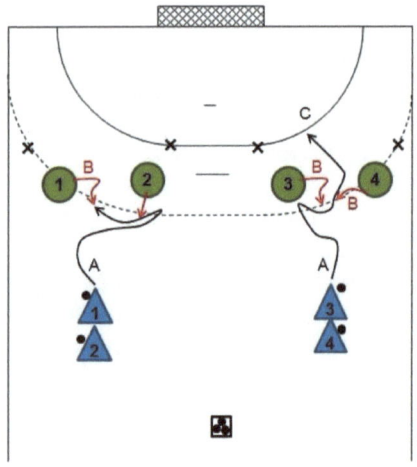

Course:
- The defending players play against a single attacking player (here 1 and 3).
- 1 (3) runs towards the defense holding a ball (A). The attacking player may do any number of steps without dribbling.
- The defending players try to prevent 1 (3) from breaking through between the two cones defining the finish line (B).
- The defending players must cooperate and get into physical contact with the attacking player.
- If the attacking player breaks through (C), he gets a point.
- Each attacking player must try to break through on each side. Afterwards, change the defending players, so that each player has played defense once (twice for smaller groups).
- Which attacking player has scored highest?

⚠ The defending players must be willing to get into physical contact and to collaborate to prevent the attacking player from breaking through.

No. 9	Preventing an attacking player from breaking through 3-on1 or 2-on-1	8	

Equipment required: 2 cones, ball box with sufficient number of handballs

Setting:
- Make teams of three.
- Define the playing field with cones.

Course 1 (figure 1):
- One team of three starts as defending team, one team as attacking team, the players of the third team serve as feeders/receivers (4 and 5).
- The defending players play against a single attacking player (here 1).

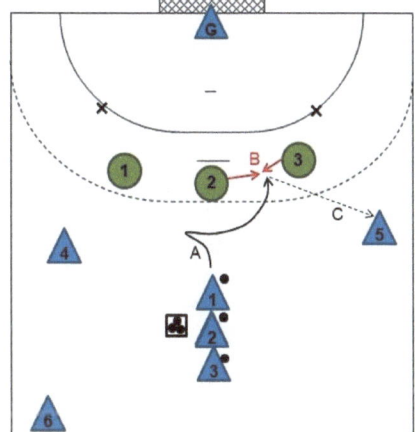

- 1 runs towards the defense (Figure 1) holding a ball (A). 1 may do any number of steps without dribbling.
- The defending players try to defend against 1 and to prevent any further attacking actions (B).
- 1 has the following options for scoring:
    o Shot from behind the 9-meter line -> 1 gets two points for each goal.
    o Breakthrough and shot within the 9-meter zone (three points for a goal, two points if 1 manages to shoot at the goal).
    o Pass from within the 9-meter zone to one of the feeders/receivers (C), one point.
- If the defense players tackle 1 in such a way that he cannot do any further actions, he doesn't get a p
- 1, 2, and 3 each play two attacks (six actions for the defense). Afterwards, add up the points.
- Switch the tasks (1, 2, and 3 become the defense players; 4, 5, and 6 become the attacking players; 1, 2, and 3 may take a break and serve as feeders/receivers).
- Each team plays defense one time and offense at least one time.
- Which defending team is best in preventing the attacking players from scoring?

Course 2 (Figure 2):
- The course remains the same; however, now there are only two defending players playing in a slightly smaller field (the defending team of two substitutes one player each after two actions).

⚠ The defending players must be willing to get into physical contact and to collaborate to prevent the attacking player from shooting, breaking through, or playing a pass.

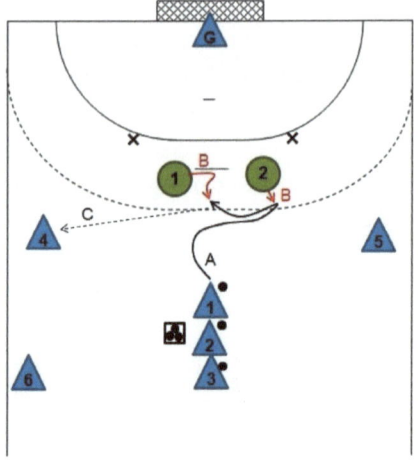

(Figure 2)

⚠ The attacking players must move dynamically and must not dread to get into physical contact in order to score as many points as possible.

3. 1-on-1 defense play

No. 10	**Ball familiarization 1-on-1**	3	★★
Equipment required: 4 cones and 1 handball per group of 3			

Setting:
- Make teams of three, each team having one ball and 4 cones.
- The players stand as shown in the figure.

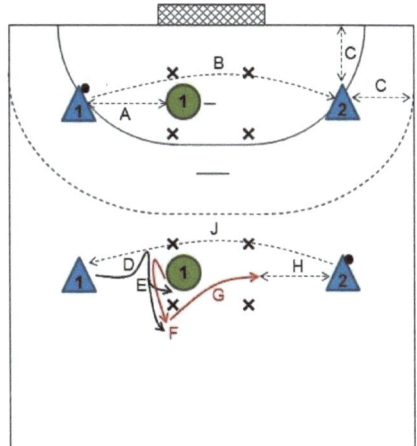

Course:
- 1 passes the ball to 1 and immediately receives a return pass (A).
- 1 plays a slight banana pass over 1 to 2 (B).
- 2 turns to the wall, bounces the ball once or twice against it and catches it again (C).
- After his pass to 2 (B), 1 tries to get past 1 and into the space between the cones (D and E). 1 steps forward into the movement path of 1 and pushes him past the cone using his arms (F).
- After the action, 1 turns around at once, runs through the cones and to the other side (G), receives the ball from 2, and immediately plays a return pass (H).
- 2 plays a slight banana pass over 1 to 1 (J) and the course starts over.
- Change the defending players after four to five rounds.

⚠ 1 should adjust immediately after the first action (F) and start the subsequent action (G and H).

⚠ 1 must not clinch or hold 1 during the entire action.

⚠ 1 should use his arms as shock absorbers when defending against 1 and push 1 backward and to the side by proper legwork.

No. 11	Basic movements and 1-on-1	3	★★
Equipment required: 1 cone and 1 handball per group of 3			

Basic setting:
- The players make teams of three; each team has one cone and one ball.

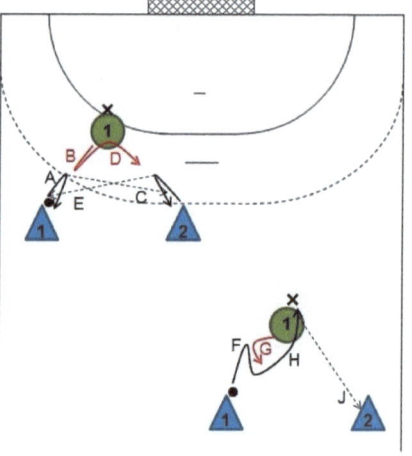

Course:
- 🔺 makes a forward piston movement (A) and 🟢 steps forward into the piston movement path (B).
- 🔺 passes he ball to 🔺 (C).
- 🟢 slightly moves backward in order to secure the cone and then immediately steps forward into the piston movement path of 🔺 (D) -> "triangle move".
- Afterwards, the players repeat the piston movement and 🔺 receives the ball (E) etc.
- The players keep repeating the piston movement until one of them bounces the ball (🔺 in the example). This is the starting sign for the subsequent 1-on-1 action.
- 🔺 now dynamically runs towards the cone (F) and tries to reach the cone in a 1-on-1 action (H). 🟢 tries to keep 🔺 away from the cone using proper legwork as well as his arms (G).
- If 🔺 is successful and reaches the cone or if 🟢 manages to interrupt the attack of 🔺, 🔺 passes the ball to 🔺, and 🔺 now also starts a 1-on-1 action against 🟢.
- Afterwards, the three players switch positions and the course starts over.

⚠️ 🔺 and 🔺 should choose their passing speed in such a way that 🟢 is able to do the "triangle move" correctly.

⚠️ When doing the triangle move, 🟢 should always maintain the proper defending posture when stepping forward towards the attacking player (correct foot and arm posture).

No. 12	**1-on-1 exercise with fast adjustment and without a ball**	9	★★
Equipment required: 1 pole, 1 bib, and 1 handball per group of 3			

Setting:
- The players make teams of three.
- Each team of three plays at a pole.

Course:
- One player starts as defending player, one as attacking player. The third player stands near the pole at a short distance and holds a bib.
- Upon the coach's whistle, all attacking players start the course in parallel:
- 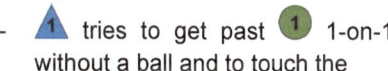 tries to get past 1-on-1 without a ball and to touch the

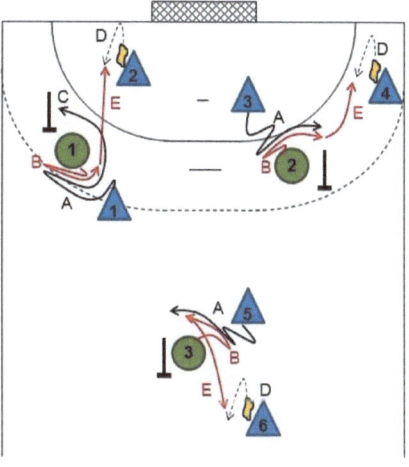

pole with his hand (A). tries to prevent the attacking player from touching the pole for as long as possible (B).
- As soon as one attacking player has touched the pole (C), he calls out "STOP".
- "STOP" is the sign for the players standing next to the poles (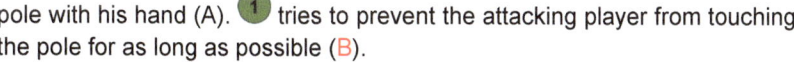, and) to throw the bib in the air (D).
- The attacking players must adjust immediately and try to catch the bib before it touches the ground (E).
- Switch tasks afterwards. The previous attacking players now become the defending players; the players who threw the bib become the attacking players; the previous defending players throw the bib during the next course.

⚠ Upon the "STOP" sign, the defending players must adjust immediately so that they can catch the bib.

No. 13	1-on-1 exercise with fast adjustment and without a ball 2	9	

Equipment required: 3 poles, sufficient number of handballs

Setting:
- Position three poles along the 9-meter line.

Course:
- ①, ②, and ③ play 1-on-1 without a ball against ❶, ❷, and ❸, each at one pole (A).
- ❶, ❷, and ❸ try to prevent the respective opponent 1-on-1 from touching the pole for as long as possible (B) (figure 2).
- If an attacking player succeeds and touches the pole (in the figure, ① is successful), he calls out "GO".
- This is the sign for ①, ②, and ③ to start a fast break at once (C).
- ④ and ⑤ defend the fast break attack 2-on-3 (D).
- The goalkeeper initiates the fast break (E); ①, ②, and ③ keep playing until one of them manages to shoot at the goal (F and G).
- In the next round, three new attacking players come into play:
    - ①, ②, and ③ become the new defending players at the poles.
    - ❶ and ❸ (who did not shoot during the fast break attack) become defending players on the other half of the court.
    - ❷, ④, and ⑤ line up again.

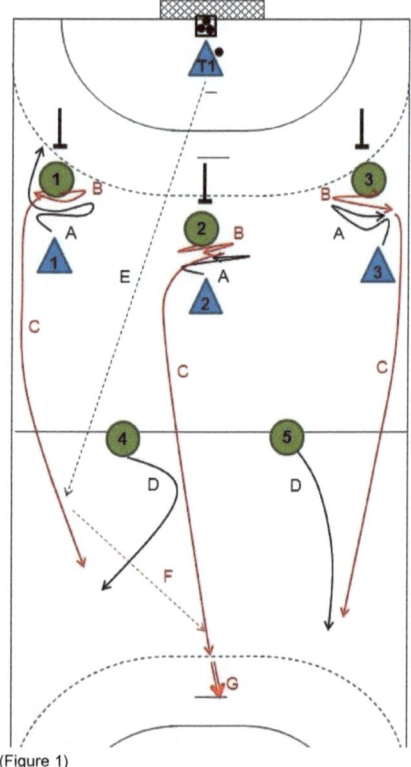

(Figure 1)

(Figure 2)

Extension:
- The fast break attack should be played 3-on-3 (one additional defense player).

⚠ All defending players at the pole should adjust immediately when they hear the sign.

⚠ Switch the goalkeepers at regular intervals.

No. 14	4 times 1-on-1	8	★★
Equipment required: 8 cones and 4 handballs			

Setting:
- Two players each make a team having one handball. They position cones as shown in the figure.

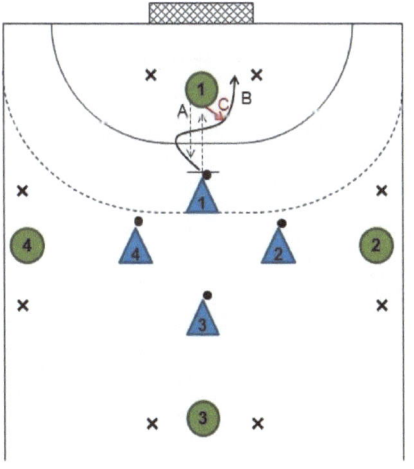

Basic course:
- All players start the course in parallel.
- Each attacking player must do five actions in a row.
- △ gets a point each time he manages to plant his foot on the line. If ① is able to interrupt the attack, he gets a point.
- The players should start one action after the other without taking a break.
- For each point △ has scored, ① must do five push-ups (after the five actions) and vice versa (e.g. ① wins 3:2 = △ must do 15 push-ups, ① must do 10).
- After five actions, △ and ① switch tasks.

Course:
- △ starts with a ball after he played passes with ① (A) and tries to plant a foot on the line between the cones 1-on-1 against ① (B).
- ① defends against △ and tries to keep him away from the line using proper leg and armwork (C).
- If ① steals the ball or tackles △, the action is over.

⚠ This drill is very exhausting; however, make sure that the players do the defense action correctly (correct posture, legwork, arm posture).

2nd course:
- Make new pairs after the first course (each player has played offense and defense once). The winners and losers of the first round now make pairs.

| No. 15 | 1-on-1 with a preparatory exercise | 8 | ★★ |

Equipment required: 4 cones and 1 handball per team of 4

Setting:
- The players make teams of 4.
- Put the cones on the floor for each group as shown in the figure.
- In the beginning, one player is the defense player, one player has a ball and stands right in front of the cones.

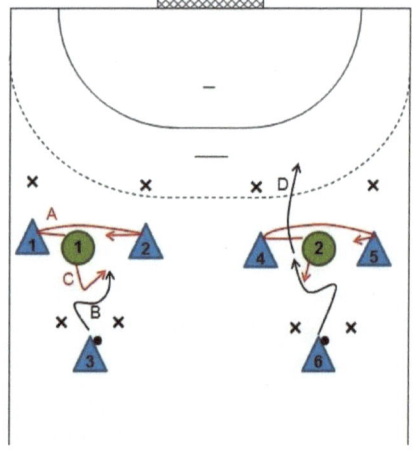

Course:
- ① and ② reach out their hands, ① keeps running quickly from one player to the other and exchanges high fives with ① and ② (A).
- While doing this, ① must observe ③.
- As soon as ③ starts bouncing the ball, this is the sign for ① to defend against ③ (B) 1-on-1 (C).
- ③ tries to reach the line on the other side; ① tries to prevent this.
- Afterwards, ①, ②, and ③ switch tasks and the course starts over.
- The other groups do the course in parallel (D).
- Switch the defense players after several actions.

⚠️ 1 should move quickly between 1 and 2 and also observe 3. 1 must always turn around in such a way that he looks in the direction of 3.

⚠️ 3 should stand and bounce the ball once or twice and then start the 1-on-1 action.

No. 16	Several 1-on-1 actions in a row	8	★★

Equipment required: 11 cone, ball box with sufficient number of handballs

Setting:
- Put cones on the floor to define the playing field and the running paths.

Course:

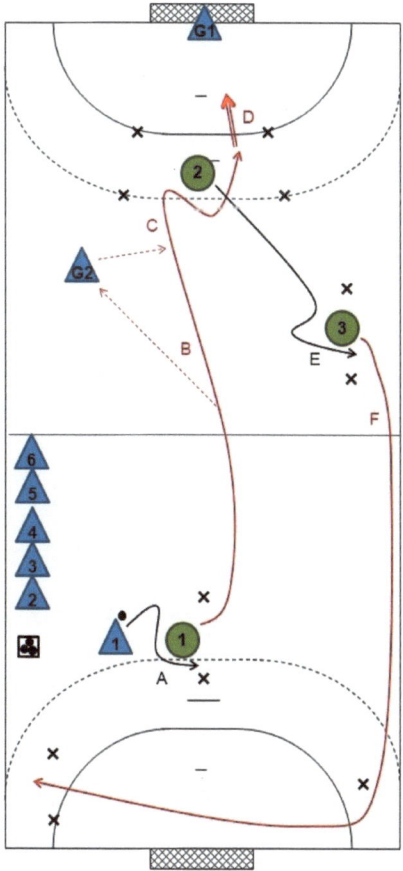

- 1 starts with a ball (after he played passes with 1) and tries to plant his foot on the cone line playing 1-on-1 against 1 (A).

- 1 immediately starts a fast break after this initial action and receives a pass from 1.

- 1 passes the ball to the goalkeeper (B), receives a return pass, plays 1-on-1 against 2, and finally tries to shoot at the goal (C and D).

- After the action, 2 starts at once, plays 1-on-1 against 3 without a ball, and tries to plant his foot behind the cone line (E). As soon as the action is finished, 3 starts to sprint (F) around the first cone and then through the cone goal. Afterwards, he picks up a new ball and lines up again.

- As soon as 1 starts his fast break, 2 starts his 1-on-1 action against 1 (initial action: pass and return pass).

Basics for the defense players:
- The defense players should act against the attacking player dynamically and force him away with proper leg and armwork.
- If the attacking player is unsuccessful during the first action (shooting or planting foot behind the cone line), the action is over.
- The defense player must then start the next action immediately; the attacking player becomes the next defense player.

Basic course:
- Each player must do the three defense actions one time (two times). Afterwards, the players may take a short break but must do 10 push-ups for each unfulfilled defense task.

 Make sure the players do the respective action in a highly dynamic manner.

 Make sure the defense players maintain a proper defense posture.

No. 17	Continuous 1-on-1 exercise with fast adjustment	10	★★

Equipment required: 10 cone, ball box with sufficient number of handballs

Course:

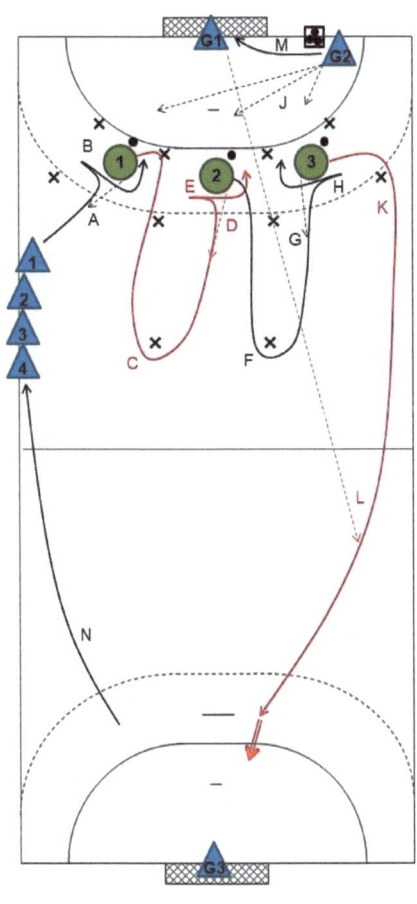

- ▲1 starts to run and receives a pass from ●1 into his running path (A).
- ▲1 plays 1-on-1 against ●1 and tries to shoot at the goal (B).
- ▲1 picks up a new ball after the action (B) and becomes the new defense player.
- Afterwards, ●1 starts to sprint immediately, runs around the cone (C), receives a pass from ●2 into his path (D), and then plays 1-on-1 against ●2 (E).
- ●1 picks up a new ball after the action (E) and becomes the new defense player.
- Afterwards, ●2 starts to sprint immediately, runs around the cone (F), receives a pass from ●3 into his path (G), and then tries to break through 1-on-1 against ●3 (H).
- Following the action, ●3 starts to sprint immediately, runs around the cone (K), receives a pass from G1 into his path (L), and eventually shoots at the opposite goal. Afterwards, ●3 lines up again (N).
- ●2 picks up a new ball after the action (E) and becomes the new defense player.

- As soon as ③ has started to run the fast break, the goalkeepers switch tasks; G2 plays in the goal while G1 feeds the defense players with new handballs.
- Once G2 stands in the goal, ② starts his 1-on-1 play against ①, etc.
- Repeat until each player has run the course 1 to 2 times.

Basic course:
- If there are not enough handballs available for the new defense players, the goalkeeper G2 passes a ball (J).

⚠ The defense players must adjust immediately after the defense play and start the next action (C, F, and K).

No. 18	1-on-1 following a preparatory athletics exercise	10	★★★★
Equipment required: 1 balance bench, 4 cones, sufficient number of handballs			

Setting:
- Position one balance bench and two cone goals as shown in the figure.
- Two defense players stand behind the bench.

Course:
- ① starts the course and passes the ball to ⑦ (A).
- This is the sign for ① to start. He jumps over the balance bench with both feet (B) and runs into the defense corridor between the two cones (C).

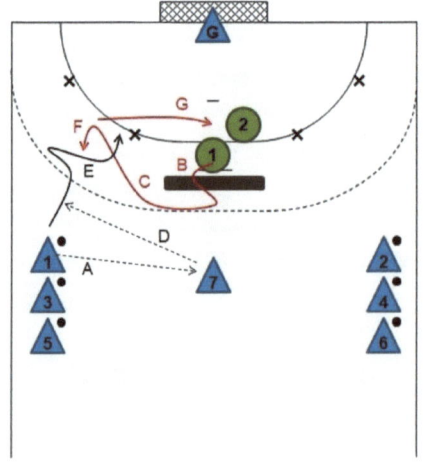

(Figure 1)

- ⑦ passes the ball back to ① into his running path (D), who then tries to break through 1-on-1 (E).
- ① tries to prevent the breakthrough (F).
- Afterwards, the course starts over on the other side with ② and ②.
- ① lines up behind the bench again after his defense action (G) and waits until ② has finished his defense action.

- Each defense player must do five defense actions; switch tasks afterwards.
- Change the feeder/receiver (7) at regular intervals.

Variant (figure 2):

- After the initial pass of 1 (A), the players pass on to 2 and back again (H and D).
- 1 sidesteps quickly around the bench (J) after he jumped over it (B) and then starts the defense action.

⚠ The defense players should obstruct the running path of the attacking player by proper legwork and try to push him aside using their arms (force him away). The players should use their arms as shock absorbers.

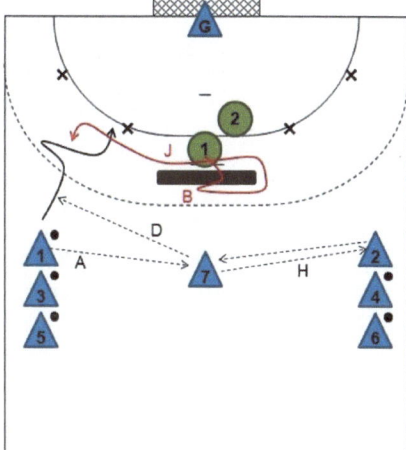

(Figure 2)

4. Covering the pivot

No. 19	Covering the pivot	6	★
Equipment required: Circle line, 4 cones, 1 handball			

Setting:
- Draw a circle on the court floor or use an already existing circle.
- Define positions outside of the circle using cones (see figure).

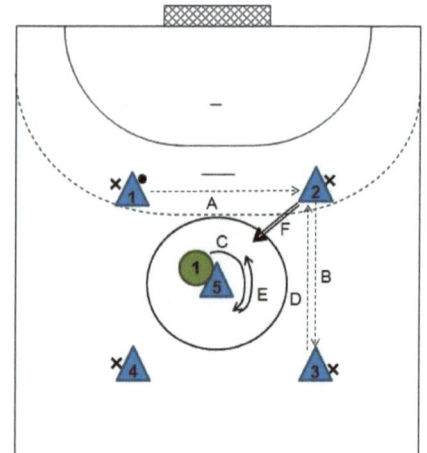

Course 1:
- The players standing outside of the circle pass a ball (A and B); return passes (D) and diagonal passes are allowed.
- ① acts as defending player against a pivot standing in the center (⑤).
- ① tries to position himself in such a way between the pivot and the ball holder (C and E) that ⑤ (F) cannot receive a pass.
- The players switch positions after several passing attempts to the pivot. Each player should act as defending player at least one time.

⚠️ If ① is unable to cover ⑤ completely, he should at least try to reach the ball before ⑤ and prevent ⑤ from catching it.

Course 2:

- The course remains the same as in course 1.
- The pivot is now allowed to move inside the circle and to receive a pass through screening and changes of direction.
- The defense player nevertheless tries to prevent a pass and to catch the ball first.
- After several actions, the players switch positions again. Repeat the course until each player has played defense once.

No. 20	Playing outside and inside a circle and covering the pivot	9	★★
Equipment required: Circle line, 1 ball			

Setting:
- Draw a circle on the court floor or use an already existing circle.

Course:
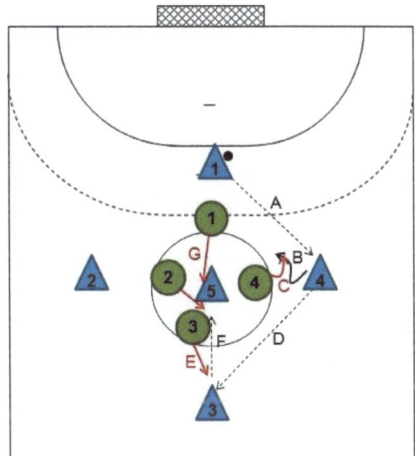

- By playing quick passes (A and D), the attacking players ▲1, ▲2, ▲3, and ▲4 either try to enter the circle (B) or to pass to ▲5 who is standing in the center of the circle (F). If they are successful in one of the two actions, the attacking players get a point.
- The defense players ●1, ●2, ●3, and ●4 must actively step towards the player who is in ball possession (C and E) in order to prevent him from entering the circle.
- The defense players who are not close to the player in ball possession must step back into the circle in order to cover the player inside the circle (G).
- The attacking players play 15 attacks; afterwards, they switch tasks (one of the attacking players stays in the center of the circle). Which team scores highest?

⚠ The defense players must communicate: Who makes a step forward towards the attacking player? Who covers the player in the circle? Etc.

⚠ The defense players must actively step forward towards the respective attacking players in order to prevent them from entering the circle and to make it harder for them to pass the ball to their teammates inside and outside the circle.

| No. 21 | Shielding off the pivot | 8 | ★★ |

Equipment required: 2 cones and 1 handball per group of 4

Setting:
- The players make teams of 4; define a line with cones for each group.
- Two players of each group are feeders/receivers, one player is the defense player, one player is the pivot at the 6-meter line.

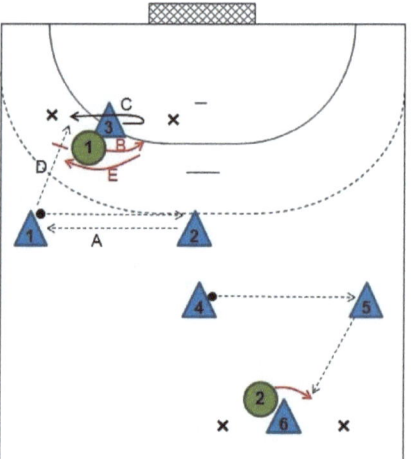

Course:
- ① and ② continuously pass a ball (A).
- The pivot (③) tries to get into space at the 6-meter line (C) and to receive a pass from ① or ② (D).
- The defense player ① shields off the pivot and blocks passes to ③ (B and E).
- ① must try to stand between ③ and the ball holder in order to block any passes to ③.
- Switch tasks within the group after several attempts.
- The other groups do the course in parallel.

⚠ The defense players must get into physical contact in order to immediately react to the pivot's movements.

Training of defensive and semi-offensive cooperative defense strategies for handball teams
60 exercises – From 1-on-1 to small group and team defense

| No. 22 | 1-on-1 and shielding off the pivot | 12 | ★★★ |

Equipment required: 4 cones, 4 poles, ball box with sufficient number of handballs

Setting:
- Position cones and poles as shown in the figure.

Course:
- ▲1 tries to get past ●1 and break through to the 6-meter line between the poles without a ball (A).
- ●1 gets into physical contact and tries to prevent ▲1 from breaking through (B).
- Upon the coach's whistle, ▲5 starts to dribble a ball (C).
- ●1 stops the defense action against ▲1, immediately moves backward to the 6-meter line (D) and tries to prevent ▲5 from passing towards the 6-meter line (E) to ▲6.
- Afterwards, repeat the course on the other side; here, ▲6 stands at the right cone.

⚠️ ●1 should get into physical contact without holding a ball and keep ▲1 away from the pivot before adjusting immediately in order to prevent a pass to the pivot.

| No. 23 | Basic movements, 1-on-1, and covering the pivot on the left and right back positions | 8 | ★★★ |

Equipment required: 8 cones, 2 ball boxes with sufficient number of handballs

Initial position of ② and ⑤ when starting the course on the left side:

- ② and ⑤ each stand at the left cone.

Course:

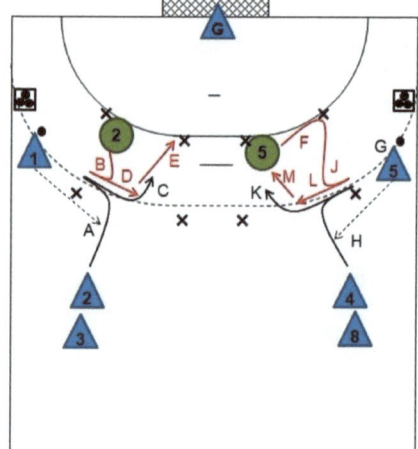

- ① passes the ball to ② into his piston movement path (A).
- ② clearly steps forward into the path of ② (B) and attacks ② offensively.
- ② tries to get past ② 1-on-1 (C).
- ② actively tries to prevent ② from breaking through (D).
- If ② manages to break through, he may shoot at the goal (not shown in the figure).
- ② stands next to the inner cone immediately after his action and shields it off (E).

After the action, repeat the course on the other side as follows:

- Immediately after the action on the other side has been finished, ⑤ starts to run towards the cone (F).
- ⑤ must bounce the ball on the floor one time (to give ⑤ enough time to start his movement towards the cone) (G).
- Afterwards, ⑤ passes the ball to ④ into his piston movement (H).
- ⑤ clearly steps forward into the path of ④ (J) and attacks ④ offensively.
- ④ tries to get past ⑤ 1-on-1 (K).
- ⑤ actively tries to prevent ④ from breaking through (L).
- If ④ manages to break through, he may shoot at the goal (not shown in the figure).
- Afterwards, repeat the course again on the other side with ③.
- ⑤ immediately runs to the cone after his action and shields it off (M).
- Change the players after several rounds.

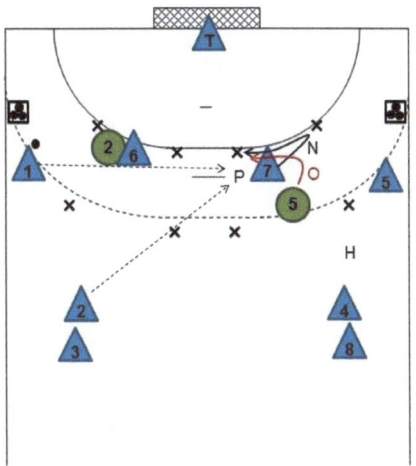

⚠️ **2** and **5** should do the triangle movement and act against the attacking players at top speed.

Extension:
- One pivot per cone zone.
- **6** and **7** may move freely between the two cones and right in front of the 6-meter line (N).
- **5** tries to prevent **1** or **2** (P) from passing, as shown in the example (O).
- **6** and **7** should move faster and faster within their cone zone in the further course of the drill and try to make a pass possible (P).
- If the attacking players manage to play a pass to one of the pivots, **2** and **5** must do five quick jumping jacks.
- If they manage to block the pass, the attacking players must do five quick jumping jacks.

⚠️ **6** and **7** may only receive diagonal passes (P).

5. Blocking in agreement with the goalkeeper

No. 24a	Blocking the throwing hand goal corner while moving	10	★★★
Equipment required: 3 cones			

Setting:
- Position three cones as shown in the figure.
- ① stands next to the left cone.

Course:
- ① starts the course and runs back- and forward around the two other cones at high speed (A).
- If ① reaches the second cone (B), ① plays a pass to ⑦ (C) and receives a return pass into his running path (D).
- ① makes a jump shot at the goal from behind the 9-meter line (E).

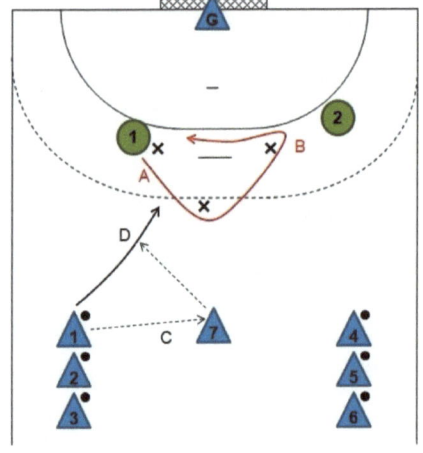
(Figure 1)

- ① should position himself for a defensive block in such a way that the attacking player cannot shoot at the long corner (colored area) and Ⓖ can already move slightly to the left side for the upcoming shot at the short corner of the goal (F).
- Afterwards, repeat the course on the other side with ② as the defense player and ④ as the shooter.
  Each defense player must do the course five times; switch tasks afterwards.

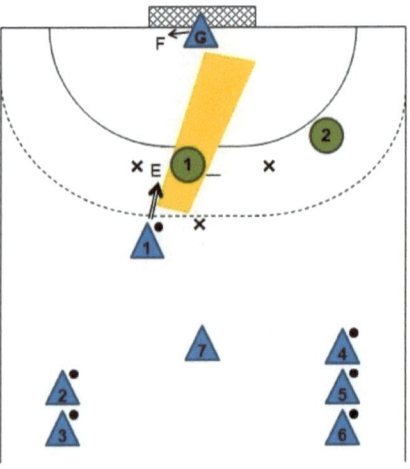
(Figure 2)

⚠ Ⓖ should communicate with the defense player loudly from the goal zone and correct his position in such a way that he blocks the throwing hand properly and covers the long corner of the goal.

⚠ The attacking players make jump shots from behind the 9-meter line.

No. 24b	Blocking the short goal corner while moving	10	★★★
Equipment required: 3 cones			

Setting:
- Position three cones for the preparatory exercise as shown in the figure – slightly further to the left on the back position from which the players shoot.
- ① stands next to the right cone.

Course:
- ① starts the course and runs back- and forward around the two other cones at high speed (A).
- If ① has run around the foremost cone (B), ① plays a pass to ④ (C) and receives a return pass into his running path (D).
- ① runs to the right side of the cone and makes a jump shot at the goal from behind the 9-meter line (E).
- ① should position himself for a defensive block in such a way that he is able to block the shot at the short corner (colored area) and Ⓖ can already move slightly to the right side for the upcoming shot at the long corner of the goal (F).
- Afterwards, repeat the course.
- Each defense player must do the course five times. Change the defense players afterwards.

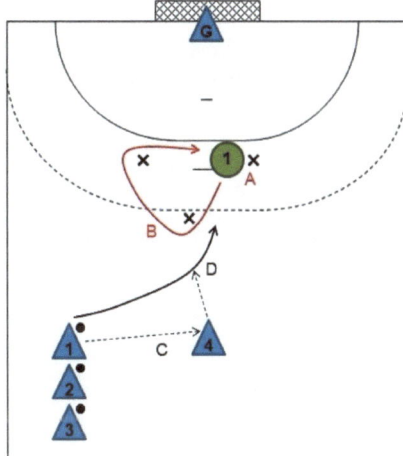
(Figure 1)

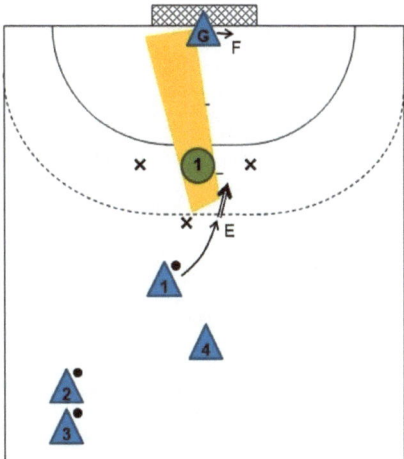
(Figure 2)

Basic idea of exercises 24a and 24b:
- If a back position player runs straight towards the goal from his position and makes a jump shot:
  - The defending player covers the long corner.
  - The goalkeeper covers "his" short corner.
- If the back position player crosses the center and then runs towards the goal and makes a jump shot:
  - The defending player covers the short corner.
  - The goalkeeper covers the long corner.

⚠️ G and 1 switch the covered side of the goal.

⚠️ G must communicate loudly and clearly with 1 from the goal zone and give him support for his defensive block against 1.

No. 25	Blocking following a 1-on-1 action	10	★★★
Equipment required: 4 cones, 4 poles, ball box with sufficient number of handballs			

Setting:
- Position cones and poles as shown in the figure.

Course:
- 1 tries to get past 1 and break through to the 6-meter line between the poles without a ball (A).
- 1 gets into physical contact and tries to prevent 1 from breaking through (B).
- Upon the coach's whistle, 1 leaves the defense and runs around the backmost cone (C).
- 5 passes a ball to 1 (D) and 1 shoots at the goal from the back position (F).
- 1 runs around the cone at the 6-meter line after the whistle (E) and tries to block the shot of 1.
- Afterwards, the players do the same course on the other side.

⚠️ 1 should initially try to get into physical contact during the action without ball and keep 1 away from the 6-meter line. Afterwards he should adjust immediately in order to block the shot defensively.

No. 26	**Blocking after a 1-on-1 action with the attacking players crossing**	10	★★★

Equipment required: 2 cones, ball boxes with sufficient number of handballs

Setting:
- Define the breakthrough zone at the 6-meter line with cones (slightly further in the back so that the defense player can run along the 6-meter line freely).

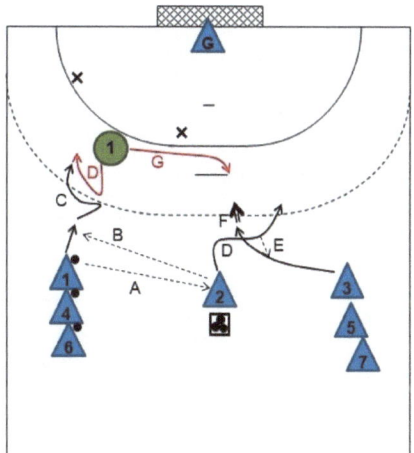

Course:
- ① passes to ② (A), starts to run, receives a return pass (B), and tries to get past ① 1-on-1 (C) and shoot at the goal, if possible.
- ① tries to prevent the breakthrough (D).
- Immediately after the shot or upon the coach's whistle (if ① interrupts the attack), the second action starts.
- ② picks up a ball from the ball box and starts a crossing to the right side (D).
- ③ takes on the crossing, receives a pass (E), and eventually shoots at the goal from the 9-meter line (F).
- ① immediately runs towards the center and tries to block the shot of ③ (G).
- Afterwards, ④ starts the same course.

⚠ ① must start the second action at once after the shot or upon the whistle and get in an ideal blocking position.

⚠ Switch the defending player at regular intervals.

⚠ Change the side after half of the time is over.

No. 27a	Blocking in agreement with the goalkeeper	10	★★★★

Equipment required: 4 cones, 2 ball boxes with sufficient number of handballs

Course (figure 1):

- ① starts the piston movement on the wing position and passes the ball (A) into the running path of ② (B).
- ② steps forward actively towards the piston movement path of ② (C).
- ③ shields ⑥ off.

(Figure 1)

Subsequent course (figure 2):

- ② clearly moves towards the center (D).
- ③ covers ② (E), and ② covers ⑥ (F).

Shooting action (figure 3):

- ③ covers the short corner in the defensive block (G).

⚠ Handing over and changing the standard agreement (defense: throwing hand corner) between goalkeeper and ③.

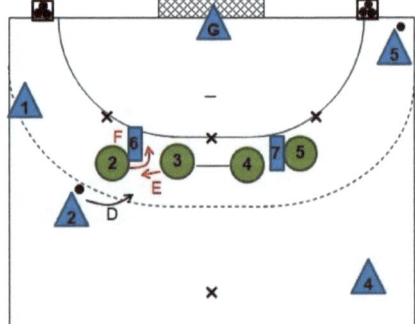
(Figure 2)

- The shooting player should be forced to shoot at the long corner of the goal (H). Since the goalkeeper is prepared for this task, he covers the long corner (J).

Afterwards, the players do the same course on the other side.

Variant after a few rounds:

- ② must decide during his action:
  - Shoot at the short corner (if ③ doesn't cover the short corner properly).
  - Pass to ⑥.
  - Shoot at the long corner.

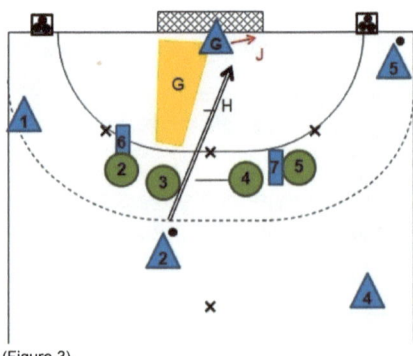
(Figure 3)

Training of defensive and semi-offensive cooperative defense strategies for handball teams
60 exercises – From 1-on-1 to small group and team defense

| No. 27b | Blocking in agreement with the goalkeeper | 10 | ★★★★ |

Equipment required: 2 cones, 2 ball boxes with sufficient number of handballs

Basic course:

- 2, 3, 4, and 6 play 4-on-4 against 2, 3, 4, and 5.
- The four attacking players play the attacking strategies below in order to score goals.
- Once they have played five attacks, the attacking players and the defending players switch positions. Which team has scored highest after five attacks?

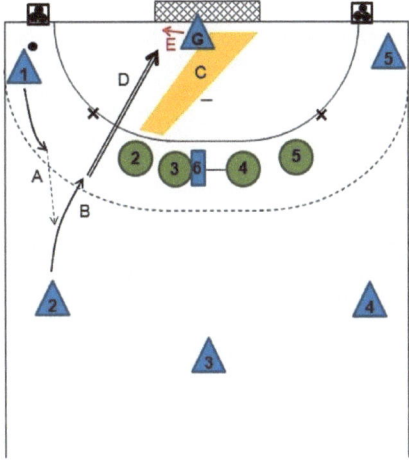

(Figure 1)

Strategy 1 (figure 1):

- 1 starts the piston movement on the wing position and passes the ball into the running path of 2 (A).
- 2 makes a piston movement towards the outer side (B); in this situation, the defense players should communicate as usual. 2 covers the long corner (C), forcing 2 to shoot at the short corner of the goal (D and E).

Strategy 2 (figure 2):

- If 2 moves through the center after the initial pass from 1 (F), the defense players and the goalkeeper G switch corners.
- 2 now covers the short corner (G) and the goalkeeper G covers the long corner, forcing 2 to shoot at the long corner of the goal (H and J).

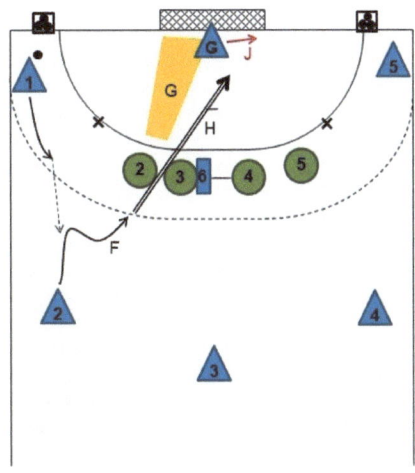

(Figure 2)

Strategy 3 (figure 3):

- 🔼5 starts the piston movement on the wing position and passes into the piston movement path of 🔼4 (K).
- 🔼4 passes into the running path of 🔼3 to the left (L).
- 🔼2 takes on the crossing of 🔼3 and receives the ball (M).
- 🔼2 approaches the goal dynamically (N).
- In this situation, the defense players and the goalkeeper 🔼G switch corners as well.
- 🟢3 covers the short corner (O), forcing 🔼2 to shoot in the long corner of the goal (P and R).

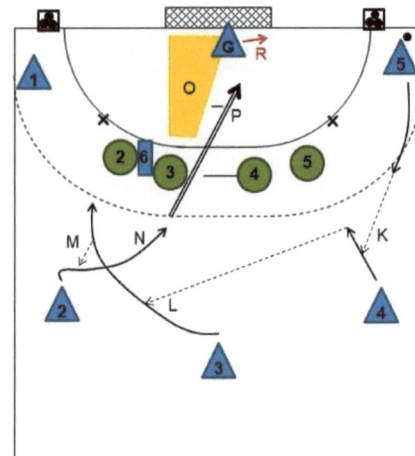

(Figure 3)

Training of defensive and semi-offensive cooperative defense strategies for handball teams
60 exercises – From 1-on-1 to small group and team defense

Category: Active wing position defense

No. 28	Pressing on the wing positions	8	★★
Equipment required: 2 cones, 1 ball box with sufficient number of handballs			

Setting:
- Position two cones as shown in the figure.

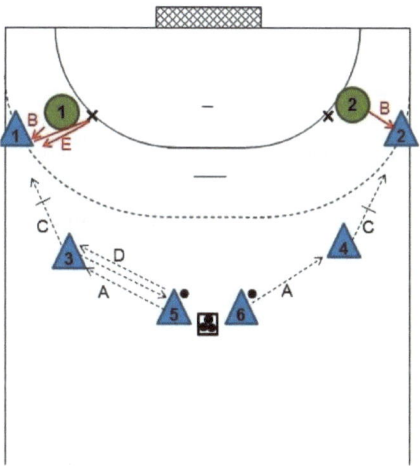

Course:
- 5 starts the drill (A) and passes a ball to 3.
- 1 offensively makes a step forward towards 1 (B) and prevents 3 from playing a pass (C).
- 3 tries to play the pass to 1 for three seconds (3-second rule); 1 may try to get into space on the wing position.
- After three seconds, 3 plays a return pass to 5 (D), and the course starts over.
- During the pass of 3 to 5, 1 runs back to the cone, touches it, and then moves forward again (E).
- The players do the same course on the other side in parallel.

Competition:
- 1 and 2 play against each other. The player who blocks the most passes during the specified time period wins.

Training of defensive and semi-offensive cooperative defense strategies for handball teams
60 exercises – From 1-on-1 to small group and team defense

No. 29	Active wing player on the opposite side	8	★★
Equipment required: 2 cones, 1 handball			

Setting:
- Position two cones in line with the goal posts.

Course 1:
- ① and ② practice the running moves of the wing players in a defense system with offensive wing players on the opposite side; ③ acts as defense player on the center front position.
- The players pass the ball several times from left to right (A to E) and from right to left (figure 1).
- During the pass from the center to the right back (D), the defense wing player who is on the opposite side of the ball holder (①) steps forward offensively (F).
- As soon as the players pass the ball back to the center and to the other side again, the defense wing players move back again to their former defense wing position (C).

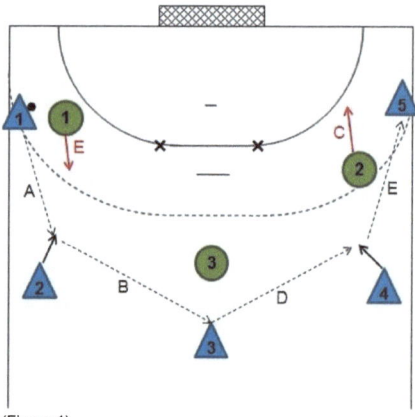
(Figure 1)

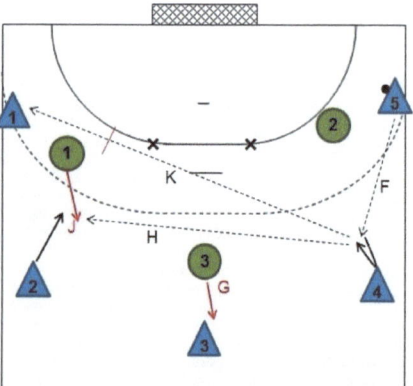
(Figure 2)

Course 2 (figure 2):
- Extension of the basic move: The players play a long pass from back position to back position.
- During the pass from the wing player to the back player (F), ③ steps forward into the passing path to ③ (G) and forces a long pass from ④ to ② (H).
- ① tries to catch the ball on his offensive position (J) (figure 3).
- ① must not start too soon, as otherwise ④ could possibly play a pass to ① (K).

(Figure 3)

- Switch tasks after several catching attempts of both wing players.

⚠ The back positions players should start running towards the passing path as they would do in a real game, even though they know that the wing player could try to catch the ball.

⚠ The wing players should try to catch the ball as close to their opponent as possible.

No. 30	Pressing on the wing positions and active wing player on the opposite side	8	★★
Equipment required: 2 cones, 1 ball box with sufficient number of handballs			

Setting:
- Position two cones as shown in the figure.

Course:
- 3 starts the drill and passes a ball to 4 (A).
- 2 offensively makes a step forward towards 5 (B) and prevents 4 from playing a pass (C).
- 1 also acts offensively (E) in order to prevent long passes from 4 to 2 (D) or to 1 (not shown in the figure).
- If the players pass the ball back to 3 (figure 2), both defense players get in a more defensive position.
- During the pass from 3 to 2 (F), 1 offensively makes a step forward towards 1 (G) and prevents 2 from passing (H); 2 prevents long passes to the right side (J).
- Switch the defense players after several actions.

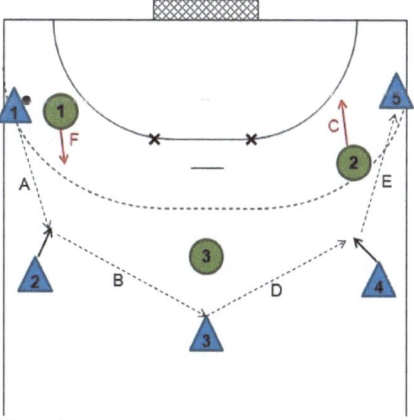
(Figure 1)

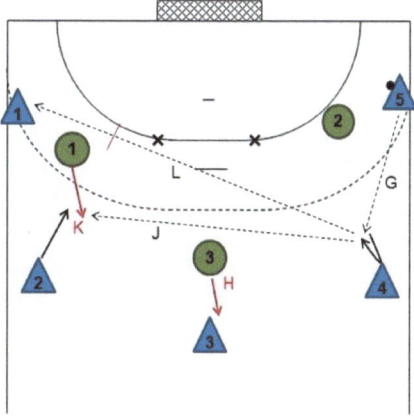
(Figure 2)

| No. 31 | 1-on-1 pressing on the wing positions | 9 | ★★ |

Equipment required: 4 cones, 2 ball boxes with sufficient number of handballs

Setting:
- Define two corridors on the left and on the right side (see figure).

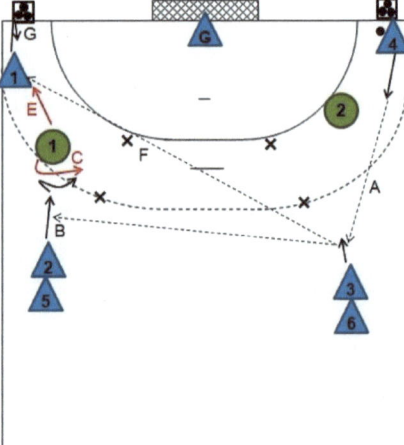

Course:
- 4 starts on the right wing position and passes the ball to 3 (A) into his slight piston movement.
- 1 acts offensively.
- 3 passes to 2 into his forward movement path (B).
- 1 makes a step forward towards 2, defends against him 1-on-1 (C), and prevents 2 from breaking through.
- If 1 steps forward too soon, 3 may also play a pass to 1 on the wing position directly (F). 1 should anticipate this pass early, move to the wing position (E) and prevent 1 from shooting or at least try to force a shot from the outer wing position.

⚠️ 1 and 2 should approach the goal 1-on-1 after they received the ball. They must not play another pass.

- After the 1-on-1 action, 1 picks up the next ball from the ball box (G) and starts the drill on the other side with 2 as defense player against 3 and 4.

⚠️ In this exercise, the defense players should not steal the ball but defend the 1-on-1 action.

⚠️ Switch the defense players at regular intervals.

| No. 32 | Defending 1-on-2 on the wing positions | 8 | ★★★ |

Equipment required: 2 ball boxes with sufficient number of handballs

Setting:
- Position two cones as shown in the figure.

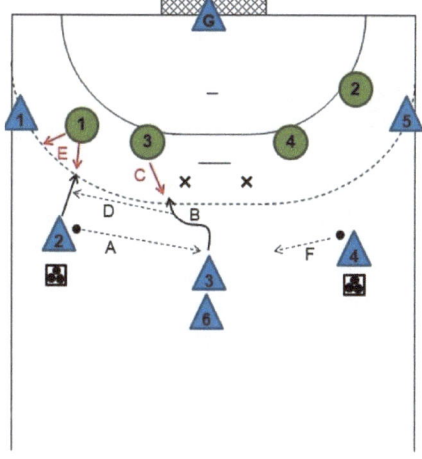

Course:
- 2 starts and passes a ball to 3 (A).
- 3 clearly moves from the center to the left side next to the cone (B).
- 3 makes a step forward towards 3 (C) and prevents him from breaking through.
- As a result of the defense action of 3 against 3, 1 now faces a 1-on-2 defense situation (E) which 1 should resolve as ideally as possible, e.g. 1 may directly attack the pass to 2 (D) or prevent 2 from passing to 1 after he received the ball.
- After the action, the course starts over on the other side with a pass from 4 to 6 (F).
- Change the defense players after several actions.

⚠ In light of the outnumbered 1-on-2 defense situation, 1 and 2 must opt quickly for a defense strategy (attacking the pass, blocking the back position player).

Category: Small group work

1. Cooperation across the width of defense

No. 33	2-on-2 with quick switching	6	★★
Equipment required: 7 cones, 1 handball			

Setting:
- Define three target areas using cones ("cone goals").
- Position one cone in the center of the playing field.

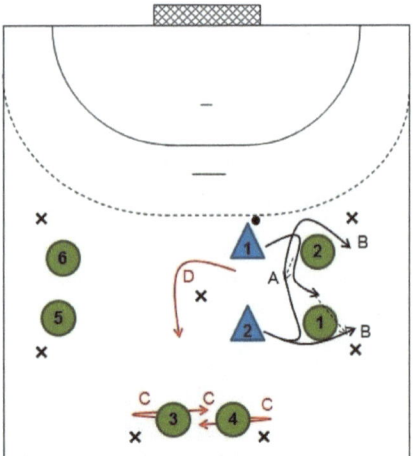

Course:
- 1 and 2 play 2-on-2 against 1 and 2.
- 1 and 2 try to position one player with a ball on the line between both cones by crossing (A) and simple breaking through (B).
- The defense players must defend the cone goal dynamically and communicate clearly (take over/hand over) in order to prevent the attacking players from breaking through (C).
- If the defense players manage to tackle the attacking players or to push them out of the playing field, they get a point, whereas the attacking players get a penalty point.

- If the attacking players manage to break through, the points are distributed vice versa.
- Afterwards, 1 and 2 immediately start a counter movement, run around the cone in the center (D), and eventually play 2-on-2 against 3 and 4.
- The points are distributed as before. The teams must do five push-ups per penalty point, e.g. each team may get a maximum of 2 penalty points (2 actions in total; one offensive and one defensive action). If the team has neither points nor penalty points (i.e. no points at all) or two points, they do not have to do the additional exercise.

- ③ and ④ play 2-on-2 against ⑤ and ⑥ afterwards. Then, ⑤ and ⑥ play 2-on-2 against ▲1 and ▲2, etc.

⚠ The two defense players should act against the attacking players in a highly dynamic manner and organize the hand over/take over by communicating clearly.

Intermediate exercise after the two subsequent actions (defense and offense each once)
- First, the players must do their push-ups, if applicable.
- Afterwards, both players stand next to a cone and start to jump with one leg quickly on the spot (E).
    o to the left of
    o in front of
    o to the right of
    o and finally behind an imaginary line on the floor.
- After the last jump, the players immediately start to sidestep dynamically towards the opposite cone (F), touch it, and dynamically run back to the starting point at once (G).
- Afterwards, ③ and ④ wait until it is their turn again to play defense 2-on-2.
- And so on.

No. 34	3-on-3	10	★★
Equipment required: 2 cones, 1 handball			

Basic course:

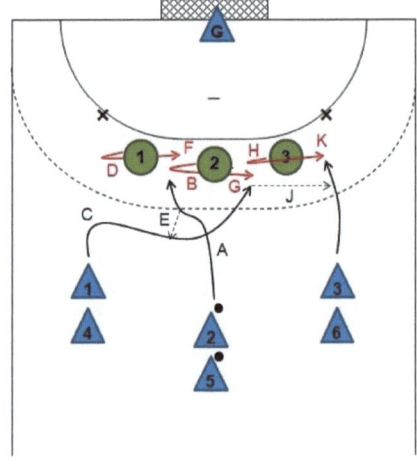

- ①, ②, and ③ alternately defend 3-on-3 against ▲1, ▲2, and ▲3 and against ▲4, ▲5, and ▲6.
- ▲1, ▲2, and ▲3 should try to outnumber ①, ②, and ③ by using simple crossing movements.
- The attacking players should not move to the 6-meter line and act as a second pivot but run out of the 9-meter zone after the crossing.

Defense action for handing/taking over

- ▲2 has the ball and makes a dynamic piston movement into the space between ① and ② (A).
- ② runs along with him (B).
- ▲1 moves along and also makes 1 to 2 steps forward.
- ① reacts to this movement and moves along a little bit (D).
- ▲1 now takes on the crossing of ▲2, dynamically runs to the right side and receives a pass (E).
- ② and ① should communicate clearly and agree upon when ▲1 and ▲2 will be handed over (F and G).
- ▲1 makes a piston movement to the right side (accompanied by ② (G)) towards the gap between ② and ③.
- ③ should reduce the distance to ② a little bit (H), but move towards the outer side when ▲1 passes to ▲3 (J) and prevent ▲3 from breaking through (K).

Overall course:

- The two attacking teams (①, ②, and ③ and ④, ⑤, and ⑥) each play three attacks alternately (six attacks in total). Each goal means e.g. five push-ups for ①, ②, and ③ (i.e. a maximum of 6*5 = 30 push-ups).
- Each unsuccessful attack also means e.g. five push-ups for the respective attacking team (i.e. a maximum of 3*5 = 15 push-ups).

⚠ The three defense players should communicate permanently and clearly define who is in charge of which attacking player.

No. 35 — 3-on-3 switch game ★★

Equipment required: 4 cones, 1 handball

Setting:
- Define two lines using cones.
- Make three teams of three.

Course:
- 🔺1, 🔺2, and 🔺3 play 3-on-3 against 🟢1, 🟢2, and 🟢3.
- 🔺1, 🔺2, and 🔺3 should try to break through and plant a foot on the line between the cones (C) by crossing (A and B) or 1-on-1 actions.
- Afterwards, 🟢1, 🟢2, and 🟢3 immediately start an attack and play 3-on-3 against 🔺1, 🔺2, and 🔺3 (E). They also try to break through and approach the line between the goals.
- After the action 🔺1, 🔺2, and 🔺3 immediately start an attack and play 3-on-3 against 🔺1, 🔺2, and 🔺3.
- Repeat until each team has played 10 attacks.

(Figure 1)

(Figure 2)

Overall course:
- Each team must play 10 attacks. For each time the attacking players manage to break through (the player holding the ball manages to plant a foot on the line between the two cones), the attacking team gets a point.
- After 10 actions, the team with the fewest points must do 20 push-ups, for example; the team with the second fewest points must do 10 push-ups.

Training of defensive and semi-offensive cooperative defense strategies for handball teams
60 exercises – From 1-on-1 to small group and team defense

⚠ The defending players should not play a man-to-man marking but act on a line to the greatest possible extent (D), step forward into the ball holder's path, and move back again.

⚠ The defending players should cover and hand over the attacking players and communicate clearly.

⚠ If the defending players manage to tackle an attacking player in such a way that he cannot do any further actions and in accordance with the handball rules, ball possession switches and the former defense players may start an attack towards the other side.

No. 36	1-on-1 and 2-on-2 combination	7	★★
Equipment required: 2 poles, 4 cones, sufficient number of handballs			

Setting:
- Position two poles on the right and left side of the 6-meter line.
- Define the running path with two cones on the left and right side of the center line; use two more cones to define the playing field in the center (see figure).
- Put handballs on the floor next to the goal.

Course:
- 🔺1 and 🔺2 simultaneously start upon the coach's whistle. They try to get past the defense players 1-on-1 without a ball and to touch the pole (A).
- 🔵1 and 🔵2 prevent the attacking players from touching the pole for as long as possible (B).
- The goalkeeper looks in direction of the goal, does two push-ups upon the coach's whistle, and then touches the four corners of the goal one after the other (C) (top left, top right, bottom left, bottom right, top left, and so on).

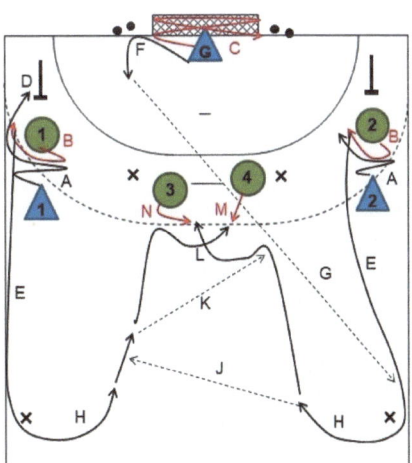

(Figure 1)

Figure 2

- If a player manages to touch the pole (D), he calls out "STOP".
- This is the sign for ① and ② to immediately run to the other side (E), and for the goalkeeper to pick up a ball (F) and to pass it to one of the running players (G).
- ① and ② run around the cones and start (H) a 2-on-2 attack (J, K, and L) against ③ and ④ (figure 3), who try to prevent them from breaking through to the goal (N and M).

Figure 3

- As soon as the attacking players have shot or the defense players have interrupted the attack, △1 and △2 become the next defense players for the 1-on-1 game. ① and ② move to the defense playing 2-on-2, two new attacking players for the 1-on-1 game are substituted, and ③ and ④ line up and wait until it is their turn to play a 1-on-1 attack.

⚠ Upon the "STOP" sign, ① and ② must adjust immediately and start the subsequent attack. The goalkeeper must listen carefully as well and pick up a ball.

⚠ ③ and ④ should communicate when playing 2-on-2 and hand/take over during crossings, as necessary.

No. 37	2-on-2 with fast adjustment	7	★★

Equipment required: 4 small gym mats, 2 cones, ball box with sufficient number of handballs, whistle

Setting:
- Position four small gym mats and two cones as shown in the figure.
- Put a ball box with spare balls on the floor.

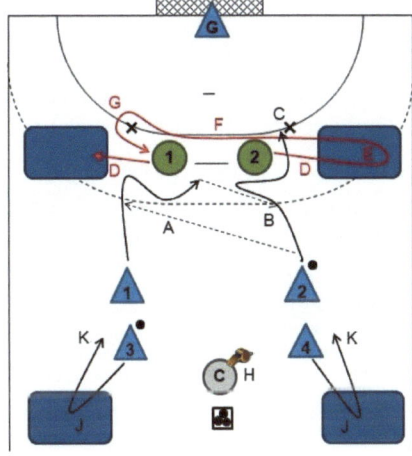

Course:
-  play 2-on-2 against 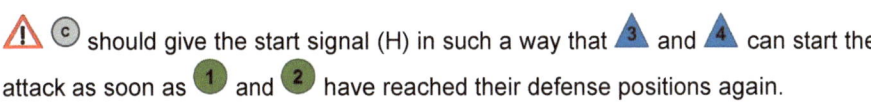 and try to get in a good shooting position while playing together (A, B, and C).
- After the 2-on-2 action, ① and ② immediately step on their small gym mat (D), do a somersault (E), sidestep along the 6-meter line (F) around the cone, and eventually move back to their former defense position (G).
- Upon the sign of ⓒ (H), ③ and ④ start to run to the small gym mat, do a somersault (J), and then start their 2-on-2 action against ① and ② (K).
- Switch the defense players after five actions.

⚠️ ⓒ should give the start signal (H) in such a way that ③ and ④ can start the attack as soon as ① and ② have reached their defense positions again.

2. Cooperation throughout the depth of defense

No. 38	2-on-2 – Defense against back position player and pivot	8	★★
Equipment required: 2 cones, ball box with sufficient number of handballs			

Course:

- ① and ② defend 2-on-2 against a back position player and a pivot.
- ▲1 passes to ▲5 (A) and makes a piston movement (B) in direction of the return pass (C).
- The defense must communicate and react accordingly:

Figure 1:

Figure 1

   o If ▲1 approaches the defense on the back position (D), ① makes a step forward and defends 1-on-1 against ▲1 (E).

   o ② prevents the pivot from receiving a pass (H), even if the pivot moves into the gap behind ▲1 (F).

Figure 2:

Figure 2

   o If ▲1 chooses the long way through the center (J), ② makes a step forward towards ▲1 (K).

   o ① must get in a proper position quickly, in order to shield off the pivot (M) (L).

⚠ The defense players must communicate: Who makes a step forward towards the attacking player? Who covers the pivot?

Figure 3

⚠ Switch the defending players at regular intervals.

No. 39	**2-on-2 defense against the Russian screen in two variants**	9	★★
Equipment required: 2 cones, ball box with sufficient number of handballs			

Setting:
- Define a corridor with cones.

Course:
- ▲1 passes the ball to ▲2 (A), starts to run, and receives a return pass from ▲2 into his running path (B).
- ▲6 tries to place a screening next to ①1 (C) during the return pass (B).
- ▲1 moves towards the center (D) and tries to either shoot at the goal or pass the ball to the pivot.
- The defense players defend the attack and try to prevent a goal.
- Switch the tasks after several actions. Each player should play defense twice in order to get to know both defense variants.

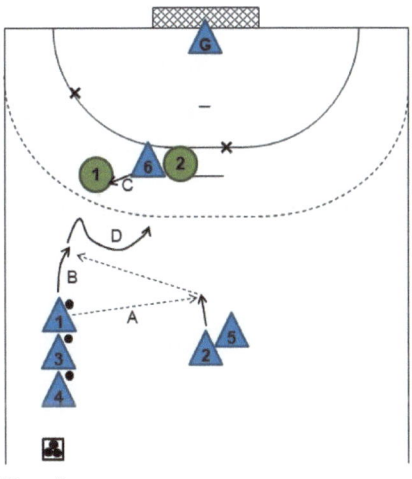
(Figure 1)

Defense variant 1 (figure 2):
- ①2 informs his teammates about the screen and defends against the attacking player running through the center ▲1 (E). ①1 defends against ▲6. When ▲6 tries to leave the screen (F) and receive a pass from ▲1 (G), ①1 must try to reach the ball before ▲6 (H), even though ▲6 has a positional advantage.

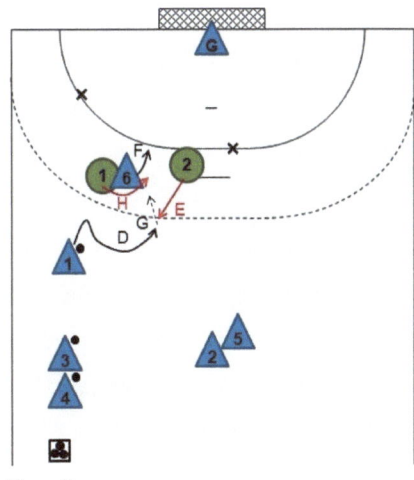
(Figure 2)

Defense variant 2 (figure 3):

- ② should clearly communicate the screening. ① tries – by moving forward – to leave the screen (J) and to prevent ① from breaking through the center (K); ② stays with ⑥ and prevents a pass to ⑥ (L).

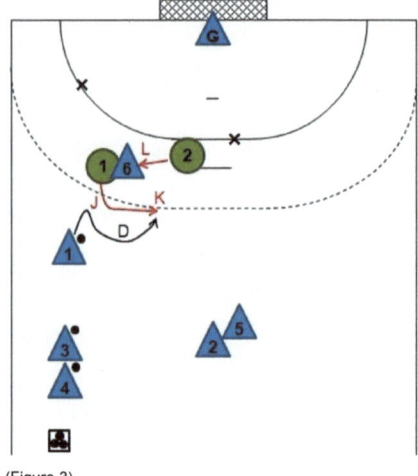

(Figure 3)

No. 40	1-on-1 and 2-on-2 throughout the depth of defense	10	★★

Equipment required: 6 cones, ball box with sufficient number of handballs, 1 pole

Setting:
- Define the playing fields for the 1-on1 and the 1-on-1 games with six cones (see figure).
- Define the running path with a pole and put a ball box with a sufficient number of handballs on the floor in the center.

Course:
- ③ starts by passing a ball to ① (A).
- ① may play double passes with ② (B) or ③ (F), tries to get past ① 1-on-1 and break through towards the goal after each return pass (D).
- ① touches the respective backmost cone after each pass to a feeder/receiver (C and H) and then tries to prevent the attacking player from breaking through (E).

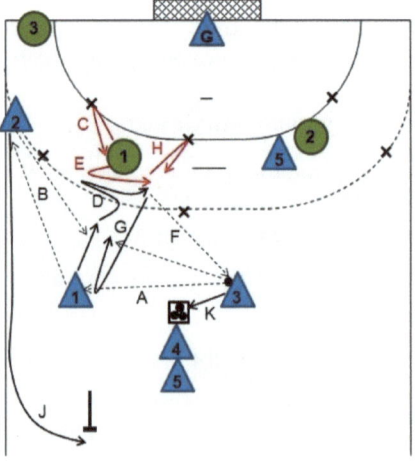

(Figure 1)

- If ① cannot break through, he plays the next double pass with one of the feeders/receivers (F), moves backward (G), and tries again.
- ① may play three double passes with the feeders/receivers in total and start three attempts to approach the goal and shoot eventually.
- After each breakthrough or after the third blocked attempt, ② immediately starts to run around the pole (J), receives a second ball from ③ and plays 2-on-2

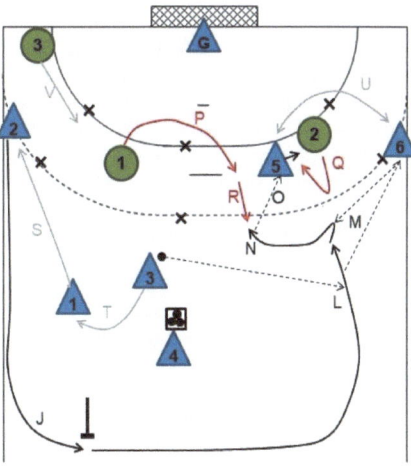

(Figure 2)

with ⑤ as the pivot (M, N, and O) against ①, who moves to the other playing field (P and R), and ② (Q).

- ② also may play three double passes with one of the feeders/receivers ③ or ⑥ and initiate the 2-on-2 action after the return pass.
- After the shot or after the third blocked 2-on-2 attack, ① moves to the starting position of ② (S); ③ becomes the next attacking player for the 1-on-1 game (T); ⑤ switches positions with ⑥ (U), and one new defense player (③) for the 1-on-1 game enters the field (V). ② may take a break from the defense for one attack and defends 1-on-1 again in the attack after the next; ④ becomes the new feeder.
- After nine rounds for the defense players ①, ②, and ③, the players switch the task all over (attacking players, defending players, and pivot).

No. 41	Defending against wing position, back position players, and the pivot 3-on-3	10	★★

Equipment required: 1 cones, ball box with sufficient number of handballs

Course:
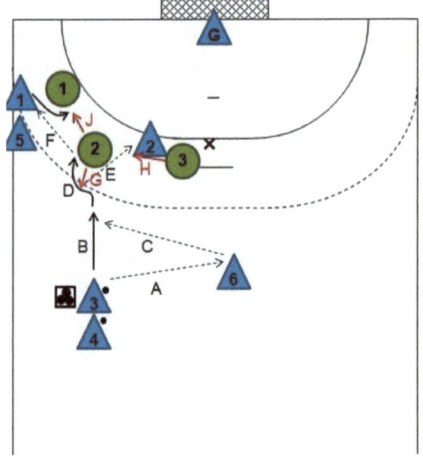

- The players play 3-on-3 with a wing player, back position player, and pivot. **6** is the feeder/receiver.
- **3** passes to **6** (A) and receives a return pass (C) into his piston movement path (B).
- Subsequently, **3** approaches the defense (D) and tries to play with the wing player (F) or the pivot (E).
  The defense must communicate: Who makes a step forward towards the back position player (G)? Who covers the pivot (H)?
- If an attacking player tries to break through, the defense players must help each other (J).

Competition:
- Each attacking team plays 10 attacks. Which defending team has fewest goals (free shots)?

 Switch the defense players at regular intervals.

Category: Team cooperation

1. 6-0 defense

No. 42	5-on-5 – Defending and supporting 1-on-1	11	★★★
Equipment required: Ball box with sufficient number of handballs			

Course:

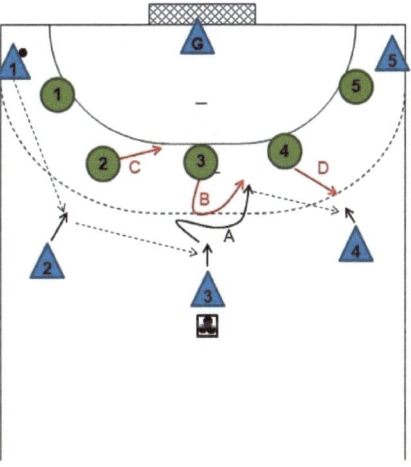

- Two teams play against each other 5-on-5. While doing this, the attacking players must keep their positions (no crossing, no second pivot).
- The attacking players try to score 1-on-1 (A); the defending players step forward towards the attacking players and defend 1-on-1 (B).
- The defending players nearby confine the space (C) and help, if necessary. They must find the right timing for stepping forward for their own defense action (D).
- After each goal (or interrupted attack), the attacking players each move on to the next position on the left (left wing moves to the right wing position) so that each attacking player has played each position once.
- Switch the tasks after five attacks.
- Which team has shot the most goals?

No. 43	Defending against the pivot in the center block (outnumbered defense)	9	★★★

Equipment required: 2 cones, 2 ball boxes with sufficient number of handballs

Setting:
- Define a **narrow** playing field to make the defense task a bit easier.
- ① and ⑤ are the feeders/receivers.

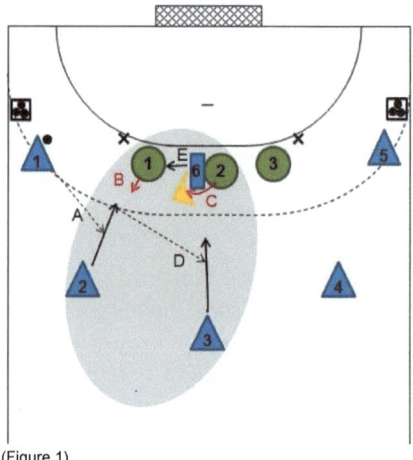

Course:
- ① starts the drill and passes a ball to ② into his path (A).
- ⑥ moves into the gap between ① and ②, after ① played the initial pass.

(Figure 1)

- ② moves towards the defense with the ball. ① makes a step forward towards the attacking player's movement path (B).
- ② tries to prevent the pass from ② to ⑥ (yellow) in this outnumbered situation (grey) by putting his arms around the pivot from behind and shielding off the pivot's hands (C).
- ② passes the ball to ③ into his running path (D) and ⑥ places a screening next to ① (E).
- ① tries to prevent the pass from ③ to ⑥ (yellow) in this outnumbered situation (grey) by putting his arms around the pivot from behind and shielding off the pivot's hands (F).
- Afterwards, the players keep passing the ball to the wing player (G); ⑥ moves into the gap between ② and ③ (H), and the course starts over on the other side.

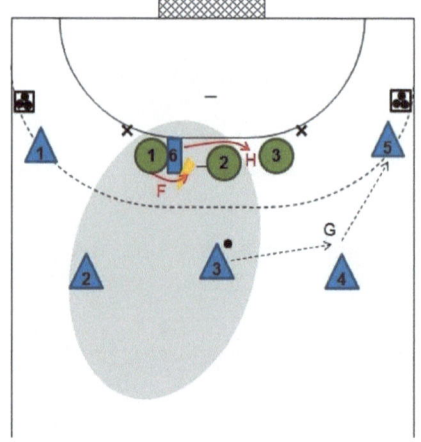

(Figure 2)

- 2 tries to prevent the pass from 4 to 6 (yellow) in the outnumbered situation (grey) by putting his arms around the pivot from behind and shielding off the pivot's hands (J).

⚠ By using this "emergency strategy", the outnumbered defense players should try to prevent a pass to the pivot for as long as possible.

⚠ At the beginning of the exercise, the attacking players should give the defense players sufficient time to get in a good position and to communicate. In the further course of the exercise, the attacking players then try to outnumber the defense players by using 1-on-1 strategies and playing with 6.

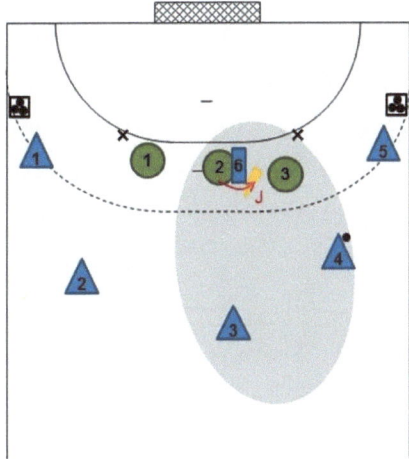

(Figure 3)

| No. 44 | **Defending in the center block of a defensively acting 6-0 defense** | 13 | ★★★ |

Equipment required: 2 cone, ball box with sufficient number of handballs

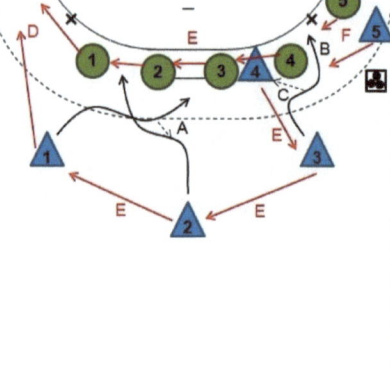

Setting:
- ①, ②, ③, and ④ play 4-on-4 against ▲1, ▲2, ▲3, and ▲4 in the defined playing field.

Course:
- ▲1, ▲2, and ▲3 may try to approach the goal by using simple crossing movements (A), breaking through 1-on-1 (B), or interacting with ▲4.
- After the action, ▲1 and ① move aside (D); ②, ▲2, ③, ▲3, ④, and ▲4 each move on to the next position (E).
- ⑤ and ▲5 enter the field from the wing position (F).
- If the attacking players score (A, B, and C), ① must do 10 push-ups, for example, when he has left the defense (D). If the defense players manage to prevent a goal, ① must do 10 push-ups.

⚠ The defense players should communicate permanently regarding crossing movements and pivot coverage.

No. 45	Defending in the center block of an offensively acting 6-0 defense	11	★★★

Equipment required: 2 cones, 1 handball

Setting:
- Define the playing field with two cones as shown in the figure.
- The players play 4-on-4. The attacking players may interact with the pivot and pass the ball, if possible.

Defense situation 1 (**stands in the center block between ③ and ④):**

- As soon as ① passes to ② (A), ② steps forward in front of the 9-meter line (B) and ③ now covers ⑥ (C).

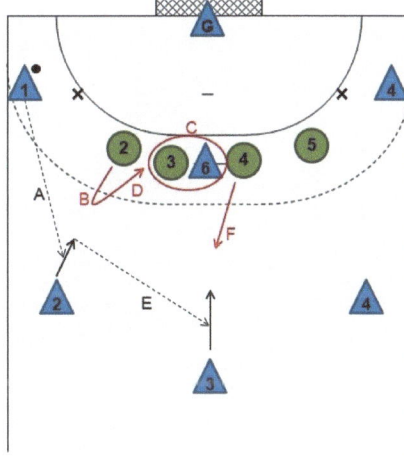

(Figure 1)

- As soon as ② passes to ③ (E), ④ steps forward in front of the 9-meter line and makes a step towards the piston movement (F).
  - ② moves back again to the defense line and supports ③ (D).

⚠ Since, in most of the cases, a right-handed player plays on the center back position (③), ④ must make a step forward towards the throwing hand of ③. If a left-handed player plays on the center back position, it might be useful for ③ and ④ to switch tasks, i.e. ③ makes a step forward towards ③.

Defense situation 2 (6 stands between 2 and 3):

- As soon as 1 passes to 2 (A), 2 steps forward in front of the 9-meter line (H) and 3 shields off 6 with his hand in such a way that 2 cannot pass him the ball (G).
- As soon as 2 passes to 3 (E), 4 steps forward in front of the 9-meter line and makes a step towards the piston movement (F).
  - 2 moves back again to the defense line and supports 3 (J).
- If 2 moves towards the center when passing, 2 and 3 may communicate and switch tasks accordingly (as in defense situation 3).

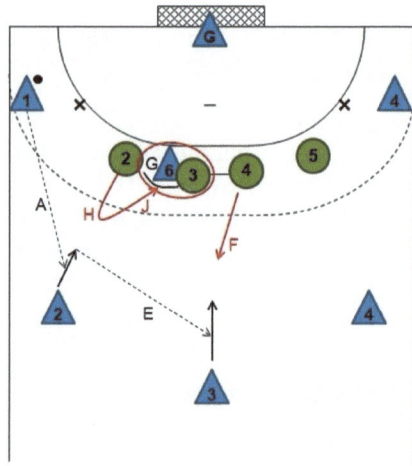
(Figure 2)

Defense situation 3 (6 stands between 1 (not shown in the figure) and 2):

- 2 shields off 6 with his hand in such a way that 2 cannot receive a pass (K).
- As soon as 1 passes to 2 (A), 3 steps forward in front of the 9-meter line (L).
- As soon as 2 passes to 3 (E), 4 steps forward in front of the 9-meter line and makes a step towards the piston movement (F).
  - 3 moves back again to the defense line and supports 2 and 4 (M).

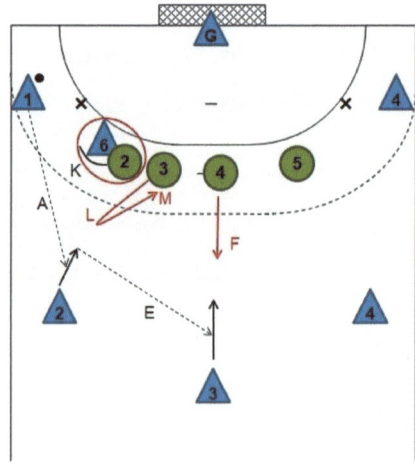
(Figure 3)

⚠ The defense players should permanently communicate the position of the pivot (6) and agree upon who should offensively step forward towards the ball holder.

| No. 46a | Defending on the wing positions of an offensively acting 6-0 defense system – preparatory exercise | 10 | ★★★ |

Equipment required: 2 ball boxes with sufficient number of handballs

Setting:
- Provide spare balls.

Course:
- 🔺1 starts dribbling, runs a curve towards the center, and passes the ball to 🔺2 into his running path (A).
- 🟢1 runs along with 🔺1 (B).
- After the pass, 🔺1 immediately moves back to his initial position (C).
- 🔺2 passes the ball into the running path of 🔺3 (D).
- During the pass (D), 🟢1 makes a further step forward towards 🔺2 (E).

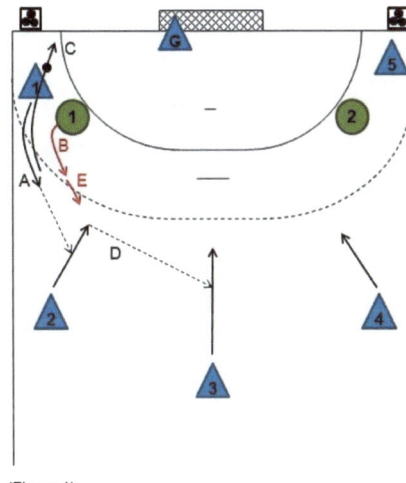

(Figure 1)

⚠️ The defense players should prevent a direct return pass and a subsequent piston movement of 🔺2, as the defense player on the half position is already moving backward at that time.

- When 🔺3 passes to 🔺4 (F) and 🔺2 moves backward (G), 🟢1 makes a further step forward (H).

⚠️ The defense players should prevent a quick return pass from 🔺4 into the running path of 🔺2, who is about to approach the goal.

- 🔺3 immediately moves back to his initial position after he played the pass (J).

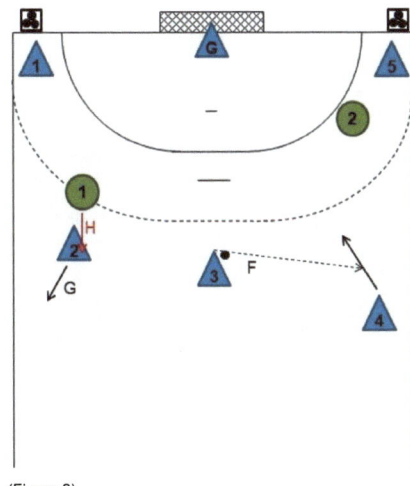

(Figure 2)

- 5 first makes a running feint towards the goal on the wing position (K), runs a curve, and receives a pass from 4 into his running path (L).
- 2 runs along with 5 (M)
- 4 moves back immediately after he played the pass, makes a counter piston movement, and eventually receives a return pass from 5 into his piston movement (N).

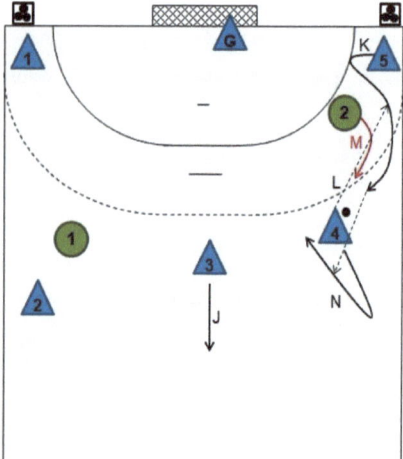

(Figure 3)

- 4 passes the ball into the running path of 3 (O).
- During the pass (O), 2 slightly steps forward towards 4 (P) and 1 moves backward again (Q).
- When 3 passes to 2 (R) and 4 moves backward (S), 2 makes a further step forward (T) and 1 dynamically returns to his defense position against 1 (U).

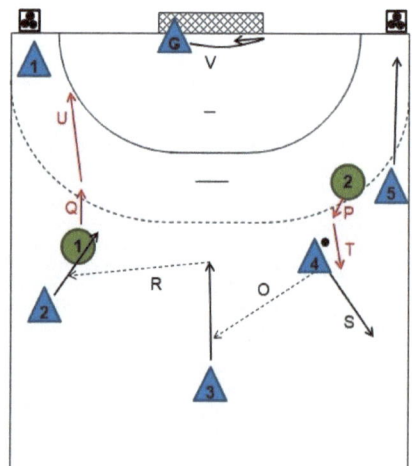

(Figure 4)

⚠ Again, the defense players should prevent a quick return pass from 2 into the dynamic piston movement of 4, who is about to approach the goal.

- T moves along with the ball in the goal zone.

Overall course:
- The attacking players should increase their passing speed during the further course of the drill.
- Switch the defense players at regular intervals.

Extension:
- The attacking players may now also try to play a long pass to the wing players (W).
  - ① must always observe the attacking players' (③, ④, and ⑤) actions carefully.
  - As soon as he recognizes that one of the attacking players is about to play a pass to ④ (W), he must move back to the wing position (X).
  - The wing player on the other side (②) must attack his opponent in such a way (Y) that he cannot play a pass to ④ without being interrupted.

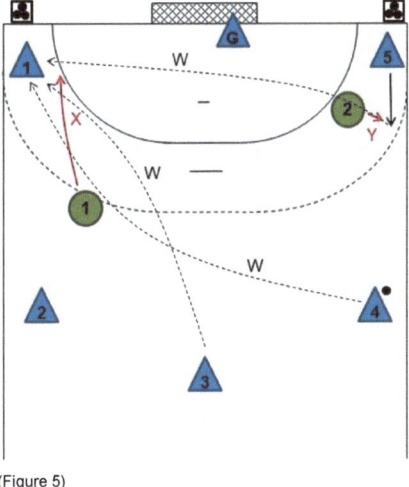

(Figure 5)

⚠ ① and ② must move back and forth with quick steps while constantly observing the ball holder in order to recognize a long pass to the respective wing player early.

| No. 46b | Defending on the wing positions of an offensively acting 6-0 defense system – main exercise | 10 | ★★★ |

Equipment required: 1 cone, 2 ball boxes with sufficient number of handballs

Setting:
- Define the playing field by putting a cone on the floor in the center.
- Provide spare balls.

Game situation 1: Wing player running along the defense line (second pivot)

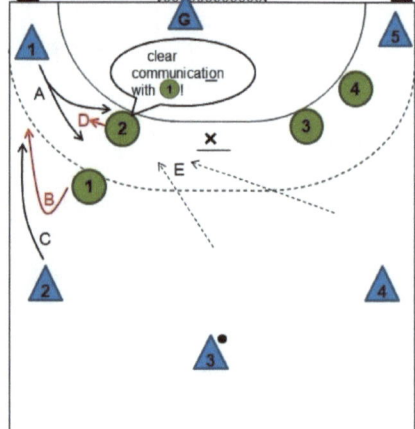

(Figure 1)

- The defense wing players act as shown in exercise 46a.

  As soon as ① runs along the defense line (A) and ① is in the far forward position next to ▲2, ② must inform ① that he is in charge of ▲2 :

  o ① covers ▲2, but sticks around him (he should choose the distance in such a way that he is able to prevent a direct 1-on-1 play, however) and runs along with him (B and C).

  o ② steps forward towards ▲1, who is running along the defense line, and defends against him (D).

  o ▲1 may move within the space defined by the cone; the attacking players may now also try to pass him the ball (E).

Game situation 2: Quick return pass from back position to back position

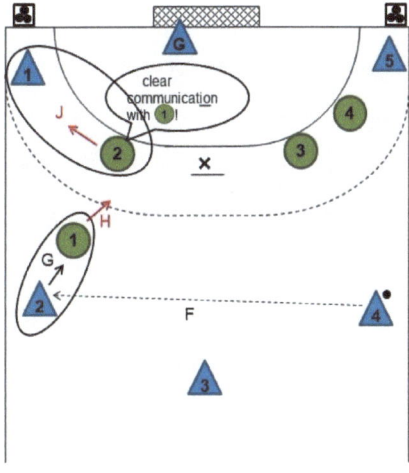

(Figure 2)

- When 4 plays a quick return pass to 2 (F), 1 also sticks around 2; he should prevent a direct 1-on-1 play, however, and move back along with 2, if necessary (G and H).

⚠ The defense players should prevent a 1-on-1 action since the moving attacking player has a lot of room both to the right and left and the respective defense player cannot be supported by the teammates next to him.

- 2 takes over 1 and informs 1 (J).
- As soon as 2 plays the ball back to the right to 3 or 4, the players act like before and 1 also moves backward again.

⚠ The defense players should carefully observe whether a wing player starts to run along the defense line or the attacking players are about to play a quick return pass. In this case, they must immediately inform each other and react accordingly.

| No. 47 | Defending in an offensively acting 6-0 defense system – Target exercise of 45, 46a, and 46b | 13 |  |

Equipment required: 1 handball

Setting:
- Two teams play against each other 6-on-6. They should implement the drills of the three previous exercises (45, 46a, and 46b).

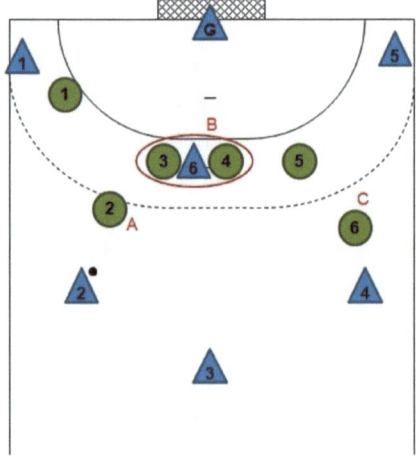

Rule 1:
- When the wing player has the ball, the player on the half position close to the ball (A) and the defense wing player on the other side (C) actively step forward in front of the 9-meter zone. However, they must prevent a direct 1-on-1 play by moving backward again.
- If a defense player notices that the respective back position player is about to break through or shoot, he must interrupt the action immediately and dynamically.

Rule 2:
- The defense players must permanently inform each other about the position of ⑥ and react accordingly (B).

Rule 3:
- The defense wing player on the other side makes a step forward towards the back position player.
- ⑥ must observe the ball holder all the time, however, so that he is able to block a pass to the offense wing player early.
- ⑤ and ⑥ must permanently communicate the game situation – should ⑥ keep the position in the front and ⑤ take over ⑤ or should ⑥ move backward again and join the other defense players?

2. 5-1 defense

No. 48	Defending on the center front position of a 5-1 defense system	8	★★

Equipment required: 2 poles and 2 handballs per team of 4

Setting:
- The players make teams of 4; each team of 4 has two handballs.
- Define the target corridor with two poles and the starting position of the attacking player with a cone.

Course:
- One player per group starts from the cone as the attacking player; one player is the defense player. The remaining players line up on the right and left side of the defense player, each with a ball.

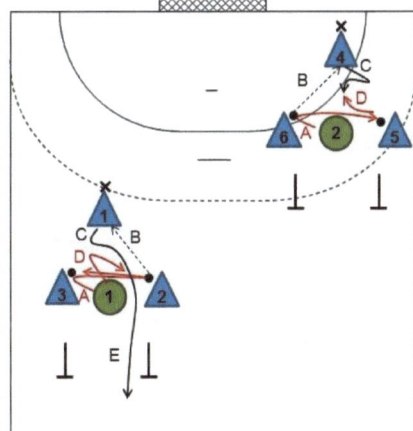

- ②and ③ alternately present the ball to ① (vary height). ① moves between ②and ③ and touches the respective ball (A).
- After several actions (a maximum of 5 to 6) ② or ③ pass their ball to ① (B).
- ① touches the backmost cone with the ball and then starts a 1-on-1 action against ① (C). He should try to run through the pole goal (E).
- As soon as ① notices that the players have passed the ball, he tries to prevent ① from breaking through 1-on-1 (D).
- ① plays nine defense actions; the remaining players switch positions clockwise, so that ① defends against each attacking player three times.
- Afterwards, a new player becomes the defense player and the course starts over.
- The other teams of 4 do the drill in parallel.

⚠ ① must carefully observe if one of the other players is about to pass a ball to ① while moving and then immediately start the subsequent action.

⚠ ① should first touch the backmost cone with the ball once he has received the pass, before he starts his 1-on-1 action.

| No. 49 | Defending in the center block of a 5-1 defense system | 11 | ★★★ |

Equipment required: 2 poles, sufficient number of handballs

Basic course:
- The players play 4-on-4.
- There is one feeder/receiver on each wing position.
- Each team of 4 plays 10 defense rounds against different attacking players.
- Which defense team prevents the most goals?

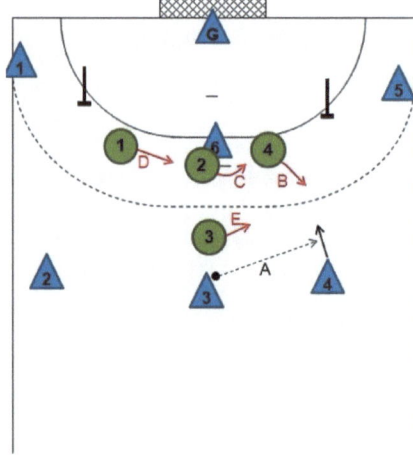

(Figure 1)

Course 1: The pivot always stands in the center between the defense players :

- Defense movement when ③ passes to ④ (A):
- ④ makes a slight step forward towards the piston movement of ④ (B) and defends against ④.
- ② shields ⑥ off to prevent a pass (C).
- ① moves towards the inner side and supports ② defending against ⑥ (D).
- ③ moves closer to the inner side (E) to optically obstruct the way and to prevent ④ from breaking through across the center and to make passing from the right back to the left back player harder.

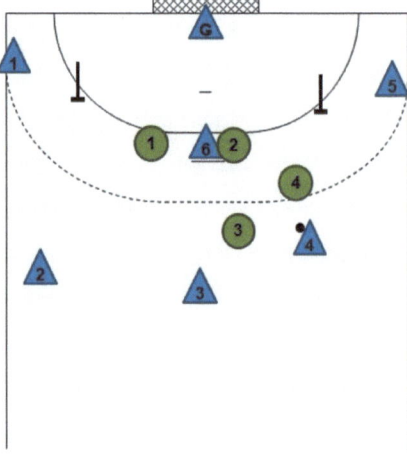

(Figure 2)

Course 2: The pivot stands on one side:

- Defense movement when ③ passes to ④ (F):
- ② makes a slight step forward to prevent ④ from breaking through across the center (G); ④ shields off the pivot to prevent a pass (H).
- ① moves towards the inner side and supports ② defending (K).
- ③ moves closer to the inner side (J) to optically obstruct the way and to prevent ④ from breaking though across the center and to make passing from the right back to the left back harder.

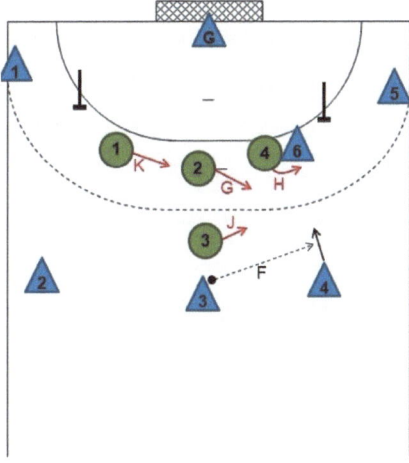

(Figure 3)

⚠ ④ must not allow the pivot to place a screen on the outer side. If ④ tries to break through on the right side, ④ must defend against him and ② takes over the pivot again.

⚠ ② and ④ must permanently communicate and agree upon who is in charge of the pivot.

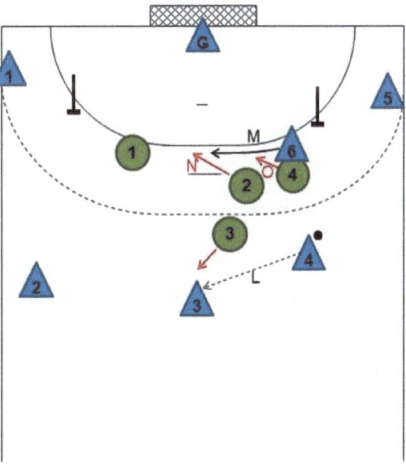

(Figure 4)

Extension:
- The players play 6-on-6. In order to do this, add two defense players. The wing players may now also enter the game.
- The wing players first keep their position. In the further course of the game, they may also run along the defense line (second pivot).

No. 50	5-1 defense system with offensively acting wing player on the opposite side in a 5-on-5 game	11	★★★

Equipment required: 2 cones, 1 handball

Setting:
- Define the pivot position with a cone.

Course 1:
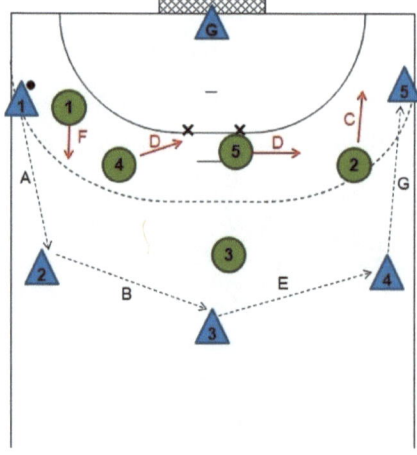

- The players pass the ball several times from left to right (A, B, E, and G) and from right to left (figure 1). While doing this, the defense players practice the respective defense running paths.
- During the pass from ② to ③ (B), ② moves back to the 6-meter line and orients himself towards the wing position (C). ④

(Figure 1)

and ⑤ move to the left side when ③ passes to ④ (E) (D).
- ① makes a step forward on the other side and offensively moves towards the gap between the back position and wing position player (F).

Course 2:
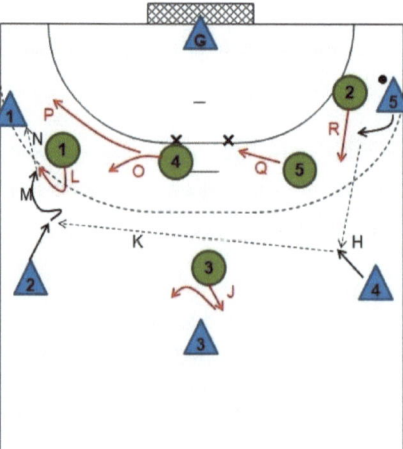

- Extend the drill by a long pass on the back positions and a subsequent free playing sequence.
- When ⑤ passes to ④ (H), ③ may block the passing path towards the center (J) and hence force a long pass (K).

① may try to steal and catch the ball directly (not in the figure). If the distance is too long, ① makes a step forward towards the attacking player (②) and prevents ② from breaking through 1-on-1 (L) (M).

(Figure 2)

- (4) must read the situation and either help defending against a break through to the center (O) or – in case (2) passes to (1) (N) – support the wing position player (P).
- (5) moves to the right defense side during the pass (Q); (2) stands offensively on the other side (R).

⚠️ The attacking players should repeatedly play long passes, so that the wing players can practice their timing when moving forward, stealing the ball and defending 1-on-1.

No. 51	5-1 defense with offensively acting wing player on the opposite side in a 6-on-6 game	13	★★★
Equipment required: 1 handball			

Course:

- The players play 6-on-6.
- The defending players play a 5-1 defense system with the wing players stepping forward on the opposite side offensively (F).
- When the ball is being passed from the left to the right side (A, B, E, and G), ⑤, who acted offensively in the beginning, moves back to his defense wing position again (D). ④, ③, and ② move to the left defense side (C); ① offensively makes a step forward on the opposite side (F).
- When the back position players play a long pass (H), ① either steals the ball (J) or makes a step forward towards the attacking player (②) and tries to prevent him from breaking through (K) 1-on-1 (L).
- ② observes the game and moves towards the wing position, as needed (M), in order to prevent the wing player from shooting in case he receives the ball.
- The attacking players play 10 attacks. Switch tasks afterwards.
- Which team has shot the most goals?

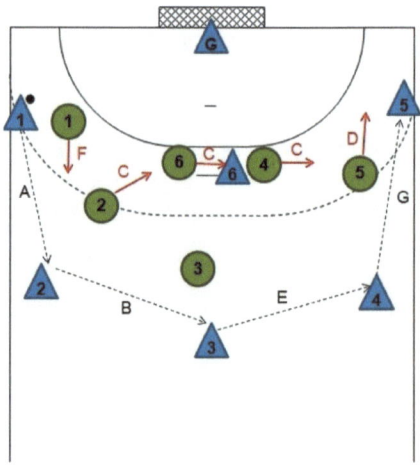

(Figure 1)

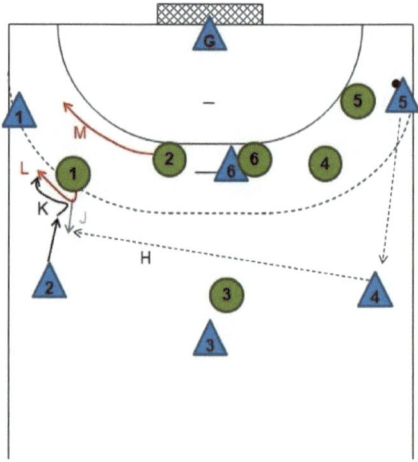

(Figure 2)

3. 3-2-1 defense

No. 52	Preparatory exercise for the 3-2-1 defense system in a 3-on-3 game	10	★★

Equipment required: 4 poles, ball box with sufficient number of handballs

Setting:
- Position four poles (cones) as shown in the figure.

Course:

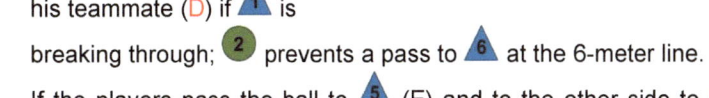

- ▲1, ▲2, and ▲6 play 3-on-3 against ●1, ●2, and ●3; ▲5 is the feeder/receiver.
- When ▲5 passes to ▲1 (A), ●1 makes a step forward and tries to prevent (C) a possible 1-on-1 action (B) of ▲1.
- ●3 moves along and supports his teammate (D) if ▲1 is breaking through; ●2 prevents a pass to ▲6 at the 6-meter line.
- If the players pass the ball to ▲5 (E) and to the other side to ▲2 (F), ●2 makes a step forward towards ▲2 (G), ●3 moves behind ●2 (H) and hence closes the gap, and ●1 moves back to the 6-meter line again in order to cover the pivot.
- Change the defense players after several actions.

⚠ The defense players should actively step forward towards the ball holder.

⚠ After the defense action, the defense players should reorient immediately and move to the side where the ball is being passed.

No. 53	Preparatory exercise for the 3-2-1 defense system in a 4-on-4 game	8	★★
Equipment required: 2 poles, ball box with sufficient number of handballs			

Setting:
- Define the playing field with two poles.

Course:
- 1, 2, 3, and 6 play 4-on-4 against 1, 2, 3, and 4.
- When 3 passes to 1 (A), 1 makes a clear step forward and tries to prevent (C) a possible 1-on-1 action (B) of 1.
- 3 moves along and hence closes the gap and helps out (D) in case 1 breaks through; 2 prevents a pass to 6 at the 6-meter line, and 4 also slightly moves along to the side where the ball is being passed.
- If the ball is being passed back to 3 (E), 4 makes a clear step forward towards 3 (F).
- When 3 passes to 2 (G), 2 steps forward towards 2 (H), 3 moves to the side where the ball is being passed and hence closes the gap behind 2 (J), 1 moves back to the 6-meter line (K) and helps defending against 6, who is moving along the 6-meter line, whereas 4 closes the gap in the direction where the ball is being passed (L).
- The attacking team plays 10 attacks, then the teams switch tasks. In the first round, the players should avoid crossing and running along the 6-meter line from the wing positions (second pivot); allow crossing and running along the 6-meter line (second pivot) in the further course of the drill.

(Figure 1)

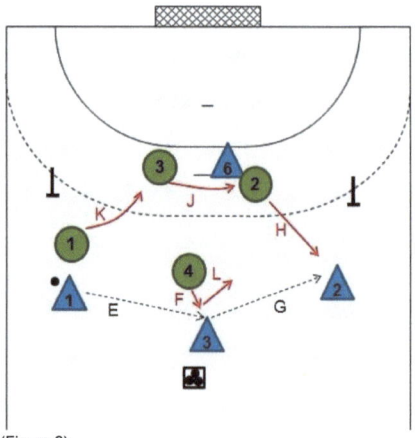
(Figure 2)

⚠ The defense players should actively step forward towards the ball holder.

⚠ After the defense action, the defense players should reorient immediately and move to the side where the ball is being passed.

No. 54	Preparatory exercise – Switching to a 4-2 defense system due to a second pivot from the back positions	12	★★★

Equipment required: 2 cones, ball box with sufficient number of handballs

Setting:
Define the playing field with cones at the 6-meter line.

Course:
- The players play 4-on-4.
- The players initially pass the ball on the back positions (A and B).
- The defending players act according to the 3-2-1 defense rules (stepping forward towards the ball holder and closing the gaps in the direction where the ball is being passed (C)).

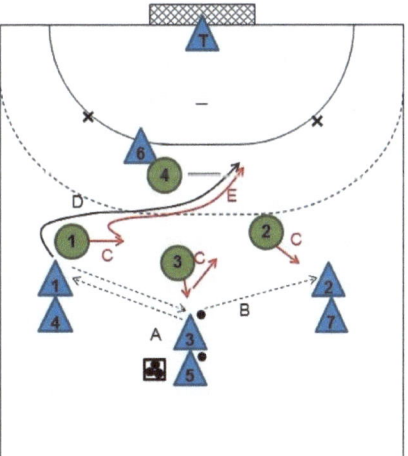

- ④ always stands between the ball holder and the pivot and hence prevents a pass to the pivot.
- One of the back position players (here ▲1) starts to run along the 6-meter line (second pivot) at any time (D).
- His direct opponent ① runs along with him (E) and prevents a pass.
- Afterwards, the players keep playing freely with two pivots until they have shot a goal or until the defense players have stolen the ball.
- After the action, the next three back position players start the next attack.

⚠ The defense players should move along with their opponent who is running towards the 6-meter line and then keep communicating with ④, particularly when the pivots switch positions.

⚠ Switch the defending players at regular intervals.

| No. 55 | 3-2-1 defense with switching to a 4-2 system due to a second pivot | 13 | ★★★ |

Equipment required: Ball box with sufficient number of handballs

Course 1 (figure 1):
- The players play 6-on-6.
- The attacking team plays 10 attacks.
- The defense players play a 3-2-1 defense system:
- When the right back player passes the ball to the left back player (A, B), ② makes a step forward towards ② (C) and actively defends against him.
- ①, who was standing a bit more on the right side, also moves to the left again (D).

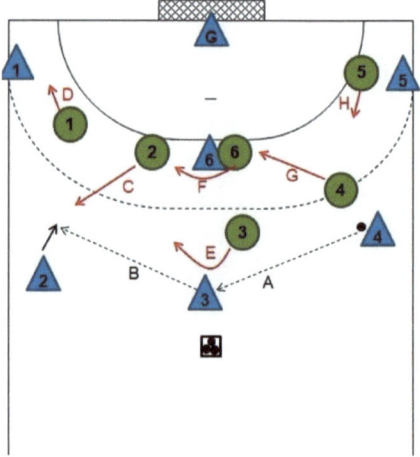

(Figure 1)

- ③ first makes a step forward towards the player on the center back position and then moves to the other side (E).
- ⑥ moves to the side where the ball is being passed (F) and shields off the pivot to prevent him from receiving a pass.
- ④ moves back to the 6-meter line (G) and helps defending against the pivot.
- ⑤ slightly moves forward and closes the gap on the inner side (H).
- The attacking players initially play freely, without a second pivot, however.
- Switch the tasks after 10 attacks. Which team has shot the most goals?

Course 2 (figure 2):
- The players play 6-on-6.
- Defense task: 3-2-1 defense system switching to a 4-2 defense system, if one of the attacking players becomes the second pivot. (A und C).
- Offense task: At least one player must become the second pivot before they may shoot a goal (B).
- The attacking team plays 10 attacks; they get one point for each goal. If the defending players actively win the ball (steal the ball), the attacking players lose a point.
- Switch the tasks after 10 attacks.
- Which team scores highest?

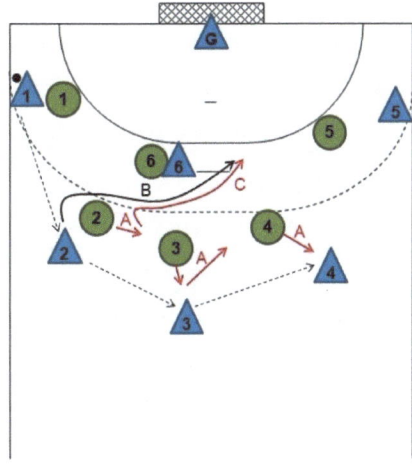

(Figure 2)

⚠️ If a back position player becomes the second pivot, his opponent must run along with him towards the 6-meter line. The defending players then keep playing a 4-2 defense system; they must always agree upon who is in charge of the pivots.

| No. 56 | 3-2-1 defense without switching to a 4-2 system despite a second pivot – preparatory 3-on-3 exercise | 11 | ★★★ |

Equipment required: 4 cones, ball box with sufficient number of handballs

Basic setting:
- 3-on-3 play
- Initial offense task: The center back player passes to the left or right back position player and then tries to become the second pivot; he should run in the opposite direction, i.e. where the ball is not being passed.

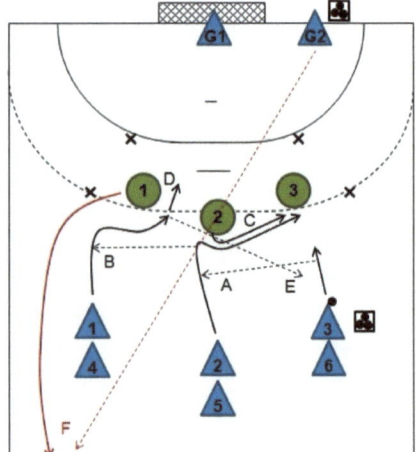

Course:
- 3 makes a piston movement and passes the ball into the running path of 2 (A).
- 2 makes a piston movement slightly to the left and passes the ball to 1 into his running path (B). After he played the pass, 2 dynamically runs in the opposite direction, tries to get past 2, and become the second pivot.
- 2 obstructs the path and prevents 2 from moving towards the 6-meter line using his arms actively (C). 2 stays in the front and hands over (moves along with) 2 to 3.
- 1 may now decide whether he should try to get past 1 1-on-1 (D) or if he should pass the ball to 3 (E).
- Afterwards, the attacking team should keep on playing creatively and try to score a goal.
- If the defense players manage to steal the ball or to tackle the attacking ball holder, the teams switch tasks.
- 1, 2, and 3 immediately start a fast break and sprint until they have crossed the center line. The foremost player (i.e. the player who runs an ideal path) receives a pass from the goalkeeper and eventually shoots at the goal (F).
- 1, 2, and 3 become the new defense players.

Variant:
- The players start the drill from the left and right side alternately.

⚠️ ② must obstruct the path in order to tackle ▲² and to prevent him from breaking through.

⚠️ The respective defense player should force/push ▲² away by using his arms.

No. 57	3-2-1 defense without switching to a 4-2 system despite a second pivot – 4-on-4	9	★★★
Equipment required: 4 cone, ball box with sufficient number of handballs			

Setting:
- Define the playing corridor with cones.

Course (figure 1):
- The initial action is the same as in the previous exercise (A). ▲² passes the ball to ▲¹ (B) and tries to become the second pivot while running in the opposite direction.
- ② blocks him by obstructing the pathway actively (C).
- ④ is in charge of ▲⁴ (D).

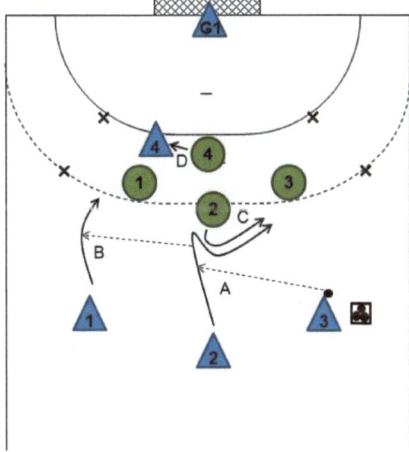
(Figure 1)

Further course (figure 2):
- If ▲² manages to become the second pivot (▲¹ has the ball), the defense must stand as follows:
    o ① makes a step forward towards ▲¹ (E).
    o ④ is in charge of ▲⁴.
    o ② prevents a diagonal pass to ▲² by holding his hands over his head and standing in the way (F).
    o ③ stands in the zone where the back position player might approach the goal.

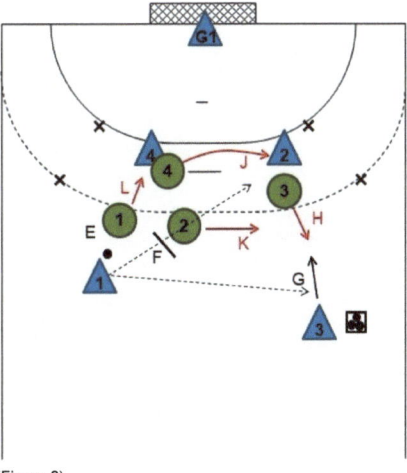
(Figure 2)

- If 🔺1 passes to 🔺3 (G), the defense players must change their positions as follows:
    - 🟢3 makes a clear step forward towards 🔺3 (H).
    - 🟢4 quickly takes over 🔺2 (J).
    - 🟢2 moves to the side and prevents a diagonal pass to the pivot (K).
    - 🟢1 moves backward and shields off the zone (L).

Offense task:
- After playing the pass, one of the back position players becomes the second pivot while running in the opposite direction (i.e. where the ball is not being passed).

Competition:
- After each attack, the teams switch tasks. If the former attacking team scored a goal, they get one point. Who has three points first?
- The losing team must do 10 jumping jacks, for example, and two sprints across the whole field.

4. 4-2 defense

No. 58	Movement paths of the defense front row	10	★★★
Equipment required: 1 handball, 2 foam beams			

Setting:
- Position the foam beams as shown in the figure.

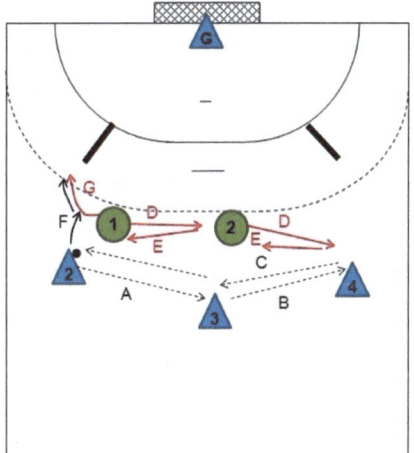

Course:
- ① and ② offensively defend against the three attacking players.
- ②, ③, and ④ pass the ball from the left to the right side and back again (A, B, and C). At the beginning, long passes across two positions and return passes are not allowed.
- ① and ② quickly move along with the ball (D and E).
- If a player tries to break through (F), ① and ② force him away as far as possible towards the outer side of the playing field (G).
- Each back position player is allowed to score a goal; however they must not cross or become the second pivot (the ball must always be passed behind the 9-meter line).
- Switch the defense players after several actions.
- By and by, allow return passes and later on passes from the right back to the left back position player and vice versa.

⚠️ ① and ② must move quickly and find the right timing to be able to reliably force away the back position players to the outer side of the playing field and to prevent the center back from breaking through.

| No. 59 | Movement paths of the defense front row and the offensively acting wing player on the opposite side | 10 | ★★★ |

Equipment required: 1 handball

Course:

- The attacking players pass the ball from the left to the right side (A to D) and back again.
- Each attacking player may score a goal; however, they must not cross or become the second pivot.
- ② and ③ offensively defend against the three back position players, move along with the ball (C), and prevent the back position players from breaking through.
- The two defense wing players (① and ④) step forward when the ball is being passed to the other side (F) and move back again to their wing position when the ball is being passed back (E) in order to be able to defend against the attacking wing player 1-on-1.
- If the ball is on the wing position, ② and ③ try to obstruct the passing paths to the next back position and the center back position (G) and hence force a long pass to the other side (H).
- The defending wing player in the front (①) must try to catch the ball (J).
- Change the defense players after several actions.

(Figure 1)

(Figure 2)

(Figure 3)

No. 60	4-2 team defense	13	★★★

Equipment required: 1 handball

Course 1 – Basic movements:

- The attacking players pass the ball from the right to the left (A to D) and back again. Now passes to the pivot, return passes and long passes across several positions are allowed.
- ② and ③ offensively defend against the three back position players, move along with the ball (C), and prevent the back position players from breaking through.
- The two wing players step forward when the ball is being passed to the other side (H) and move back again to their wing position when the ball is being passed back (E) in order to be able to defend against the attacking wing player 1-on-1.

(Figure 1)

- ④ and ⑥ move to the side where the ball is being passed in order to help in case a back player or a wing player tries to break through (F) and agree upon who is in charge of covering the pivot (G).
- If the ball is on the wing position, ② and ③ try to obstruct the passing paths to the next back position and the center back position (J) and hence force a long pass to the other side (K).
- The defending wing player in the front (①) must try to catch the ball (L).

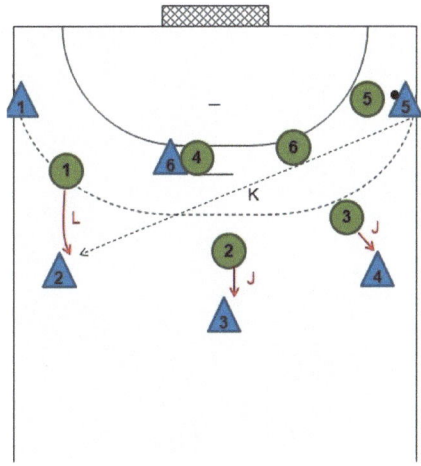

(Figure 2)

Course 2:
- Each attacking player may try to score a goal.
- The attacking players do offensive piston movements, attack 1-on-1, and play parallel passes.
- The defending players try to prevent goals while playing a 4-2 defense system and increase the pressure on the attacking players in order to provoke a mistake.

Course 3:
- The attacking players are also allowed to cross and become the second pivot.
- The defending players try to resolve these special situations.

Editor's note

JÖRG MADINGER, born in Heidelberg (Germany) in 1970

July 2014 (further training): 3-day coaching workshop: "Basic components of goalkeeper training", held by the **German Handball Association (Deutscher Handballbund, DHB)**
Lecturers: Michael Neuhaus, Renate Schubert, Marco Stange, Norbert Potthoff, Olaf Gritz, Andreas Thiel, Henning Fritz

May 2014 (further training): 3-day coaching further training during the VELUX EHF Final4, held by the **German Handball Coaching Association (Deutsche Handball Trainer Vereinigung, DHTV)/DHB**
Lecturers: Jochen Beppler (DHB coach), Christian vom Dorff (DHB referee), Mark Dragunski (coach of TuSEM Essen, Germany), Klaus-Dieter Petersen (DHB coach), Manolo Cadenas (coach of the Spanish national team)

May 2013 (further training): 3-day coaching further training during the VELUX EHF Final4, held by the **DHTV/DHB**
Lecturers: Prof. Dr. Carmen Borggrefe (University of Stuttgart, Germany), Klaus-Dieter Petersen (DHB coach), Dr. Georg Froese (sports psychologist), Jochen Beppler (DHB base camp coach), Carsten Alisch (young talents' hockey coach)

Since July 2012: A-License, DHB

Since February 2011: Handball club trainings, coaching (training and competitive areas)

November 2011: Foundation of the Handball Specialist Publishing Company (Handball Fachverlag) (handall-uebungen.de, Handball Practice and Special Handball Practice)

May 2009: Foundation of the handball online platform handball-uebungen.de

2008-2010: Youth coordinator and youth coach, SG Leutershausen (Germany)

Since 2006: B-License

Editor's note

In 1995, a friend convinced me to join him in coaching a handball youth team (male, under 13 years of age).

This was the beginning of my career as a team handball coach. Ever since I enjoyed working as a coach and had high requirements concerning my exercises. Soon, the standard pool of exercises wasn't enough for me anymore and I started to modify and develop drills myself.

Today, I coach a broad range of youth and adult teams with different performance levels and adjust my training units to the individual needs of the teams.

A few years ago, I started selling my exercises and drills online at handball-uebungen.de. Since, in handball training, there is a tendency towards a general athletic training that focuses on coordination work – especially in the training of youth teams –, a large number of my games and exercises can be applied to other sports as well.

Get inspired by the various game concepts, be creative, and rely on your own experiences!

Yours sincerely,
Jörg Madinger

Further reference books published by DV Concept

From warm-up to handball team play – 75 exercises for every handball training unit

By making your training units more diverse, you can increase the players' motivation, since you consistently offer new approaches to improve and refine familiar movement sequences. In this book, you will find inspiring exercises you can apply during each phase of your everyday team handball training – from warm-up and goalkeeper warm-up shooting to the common contents of the main phase and the closing games. Each exercise is illustrated and described in an easy, comprehensible manner. Specific notes give you tips on what you need to be aware of.

This book deals with the following key subjects:

Warm-up:
- Basic warm-up
- Short warm-up games
- Sprint contests
- Coordination
- Ball familiarization
- Goalkeeper warm-up shooting

Basic exercises, basic play, and target play:
- Offense/series of shots
- General offense
- Fast throw-off
- 1st and 2nd wave
- Defensive action
- Closing games
- Endurance

At the end of this book, you will find an entire methodological training unit. The objective of this training unit is to improve shooting and quick decision-making under pressure.

Minihandball training and handball training for young kids (5 training units)

Minihandball training and handball training for kids is different from handball training for older players and considerably different from handball training for competitive players. During their first contact with "handball", kids should be familiarized with the ball in a playful way. They should be taught that being active, doing sports, playing together, and even playing against each other is fun.

This book contains a short introduction to handball for kids and young children and its special characteristics as well as example exercises which help to make your training units interesting and more diverse.

Following this, there are five complete training units of different difficulty levels that focus on the basic handball techniques (dribbling, passing, catching, shooting, and defending in a game with opponents). The kids are playfully introduced to the subsequent handball-specific basics. At the same time, particular attention is payed to general physical experience and the development of coordination skills.

The exercises are illustrated and described in an easy, comprehensible manner. They can be immediately integrated in every training unit. By using the given training variants, you can easily adjust the difficulty level of the training units to the respective target group. The variants should also encourage you to modify and further develop the exercises to make each training unit a new and more diverse experience for the children.

Passing and catching while moving – 60 exercises for each handball training unit

Passing and catching are two basic handball techniques which must be trained and improved continuously. These 60 practical exercises offer you various options to train passing and catching in a challenging and diverse manner. The exercises particularly focus on improving passing and catching skills even during highly dynamic movements. The drills therefore combine new running paths and movements similar to real game situations.

The exercises are illustrated and described in an easy, comprehensible manner. They can be immediately integrated in every training unit. Various difficulty and complexity levels allow for adjustment of the passing and catching drills to each age group.

Effective goalkeeper warm-up shooting – 60 exercises for every handball unit

Goalkeeper warm-up shooting is essential for almost every training unit. These 60 warm-up shooting exercises provide you with a variety of ideas to make the warm-up shooting challenging and diverse, both for the goalkeepers and the field players. The exercises particularly focus on improving the players' dynamics even during the warm-up shooting.

The exercises are illustrated and described in an easy, comprehensible manner. They can be immediately integrated in every training unit. Whether you combine the exercises with additional coordination drills or use them as an introduction to the main part – various difficulty levels allow for adjustment of the warm-up shooting to each training unit and age group.

Competitive games for your everyday handball training – 60 exercises for each age-group

Handball needs quick and correct decisions in each game situation. This can be trained playfully and diversely through handball-specific games. These 60 exercises are divided into seven categories and train the playing skills.

The book deals with the following subjects:
- Team ball variants
- Team play with different targets
- Tag games
- Sprint and relay race games
- Ball throwing and transportation games
- Games from other types of sports
- Complex closing game variants

The exercises are illustrated and described in an easy, comprehensible manner. They can be immediately integrated in every training unit. Various difficulty levels, additional notes, and possible variations allow for adjustment to each age group.

Paperback from the Handball Practice series (Handball Praxis) (five training units each)

Handball Practice 11 – Extensive and diverse athletics training

Handball Practice 14 – Interaction of back position players with the pivot – Shifting, Screening, and Using the Russian Screen

For further reference and e-books visit us at:
www.handball-uebungen.de

www.ingramcontent.com/pod-product-compliance
Lightning Source LLC
Chambersburg PA
CBHW041802160426
43191CB00001B/15